Character
Education

Handling Teamwork and Respect for Others

Character Education

Character Education

Handling Teamwork and Respect for Others

TARA WELTY

INTRODUCTION BY CONSULTING EDITORS
Madonna M. Murphy, Ph.D.
University of St. Francis
and **Sharon L. Banas**
former Values Education Coordinator,
Sweet Home Central School District, New York

CHELSEA HOUSE
PUBLISHERS
An imprint of Infobase Publishing

Character Education: Handling Teamwork and Respect for Others

Copyright © 2009 by Infobase Publishing

Chelsea House
An imprint of Infobase Publishing
132 West 31st Street
New York NY 10001

Library of Congress Cataloging-in-Publication Data

Welty, Tara.
 Handling teamwork and respect for others / Tara Welty.
   p. cm.—(Character education)
 Includes bibliographical references and index.
 ISBN 978-1-60413-117-8 (hardcover)
 1. Respect for persons. 2. Small groups. I. Title. II. Series.
BJ1533.R42W45 2009
 179'.9—dc22   2008025308

Chelsea House books are available at special discounts when purchased in bulk quantities for businesses, associations, institutions, or sales promotions. Please call our Special Sales Department in New York at (212) 967-8800 or (800) 322-8755.

You can find Chelsea House on the World Wide Web at
http://www.chelseahouse.com

Text design by Annie O'Donnell
Cover design by Takeshi Takahashi

Printed in the United States

Bang NMSG 10 9 8 7 6 5 4 3 2 1

This book is printed on acid-free paper.

CONTENTS

INTRODUCTION

On February 14, 2008, as these books were being edited, a shooting occurred at Northern Illinois University (NIU) in DeKalb, Illinois. A former NIU graduate student, dressed in black and armed with a shotgun and two handguns, opened fire from the stage of a lecture hall. The shooter killed five students and injured 16 others before committing suicide. What could have led someone to do this? Could it have been prevented?

When the shooting started, student Dan Parmenter and his girlfriend, Lauren Debrauwere, who was sitting next to him, dropped to the floor between the rows of seats. Dan covered Lauren with his body, held her hand, and began praying. The shield of Dan's body saved Lauren's life, but Dan was fatally wounded. In that hall, on February 14, 2008—Valentine's Day—one person's deed was horrific and filled with hate; another's was heroic and loving.

The purpose of this series of books is to help prevent the occurrence of this kind of violence by offering readers the character education and social and emotional skills they need to control their emotions and make good moral choices. This series includes books on topics such as coping with bullying, conflicts, peer pressure, prejudice, anger and frustration, and numerous responsibilities, as well as learning how to handle teamwork and respect for others, be fair and honest, and be a good leader and decision-maker.

In his 1992 book, *Why Johnny Can't Tell Right from Wrong*,[1] William Kilpatrick coined the term "moral illiteracy" and dedicated a whole chapter to it. Today, as he points out, people often do not recognize when they are in a situation that calls for a moral choice, and they are not able to define what is right and what is wrong in that situation. The California-based Josephson Institute of Ethics agrees with these concerns. The institute states that we have a "character deficit" in our society today and points out that increasing numbers of young people across the United States—from well-to-do as well as disadvantaged backgrounds—demonstrate reckless disregard for fundamental standards of ethical conduct.

According to the 2006 *Josephson Institute Report Card on the Ethics of American Youth*, our children are at risk. This report sets forth the results of a biannual written survey completed in 2006 by more than 36,000 high school students across the country. The compilers of the report found that 82 percent of the students surveyed admitted that they had lied to a parent about something significant within the previous year. Sixty percent admitted to having cheated during a test at school, and 28 percent admitted to having stolen something from a store.[2] (Various books in this series will tell of other findings in this report.) Clearly, helping young people to develop character is a need of national importance.

The United States Congress agrees. In 1994, in the joint resolution that established National Character Counts Week, Congress declared that "the character of a nation is only as strong as the character of its individual citizens." The resolution also stated that "people do not automatically develop good character and, therefore, conscientious efforts must be made by youth-influencing institutions . . . to help young people develop the essential traits and characteristics that comprise good character."[3]

Many stories can be told of people who have defended our nation with character. One of the editors of this series knew one such young man named Jason Dunham. On April 24, 2004, Corporal Jason L. Dunham was serving with the United States Marines in Iraq. As Corporal Dunham's squad was conducting a reconnaissance mission, the men heard sounds of rocket-propelled grenades and small arms fire. Corporal

Dunham led a team of men toward that fire to assist their battalion commander's ambushed convoy. An insurgent leaped out at Corporal Dunham, and he saw the man release a grenade. Corporal Dunham alerted his team and immediately covered the grenade with his helmet and his body. He lost his own life, but he saved the lives of others on his team.

In January 2007, the Dunham family traveled to Washington, D.C., where President George W. Bush presented them with Corporal Dunham's posthumously awarded Congressional Medal of Honor. In the words of the Medal of Honor citation, "By his undaunted courage, intrepid fighting spirit, and unwavering devotion to duty, Corporal Dunham gallantly gave his life for his country."[4]

Thomas Lickona, the author of several books including *Educating for Character* and *Character Matters*, explains that the premise of character education is that there are objectively good human qualities—virtues—that are enduring moral truths. Courage, fortitude, integrity, caring, citizenship, and trustworthiness are just a few examples. These moral truths transcend religious, cultural, and social differences and help us to distinguish right from wrong. They are rooted in our human nature. They tell us how we should act with other human beings to promote human dignity and build a well-functioning and civil society—a society in which everyone lives by the golden rule.[5]

To develop his or her character, a person must understand core virtues, care about them, and act upon them. This series of books aims to help young readers *want* to become people of character. The books will help young people understand such core ethical values as fairness, honesty, responsibility, respect, tolerance of others, fortitude, self-discipline, teamwork, and leadership. By offering examples of people today and notable figures in history who live and have lived these virtues, these books will inspire young readers to develop these traits in themselves.

Finally, through these books, young readers will see that if they act on these moral truths, they will make good choices.

They will be able to deal with frustration and anger, manage conflict resolution, overcome prejudice, handle peer pressure, and deal with bullying. The result, one hopes, will be middle schools, high schools, and neighborhoods in which young people care about one another and work with their classmates and neighbors to develop team spirit.

Character development is a lifelong task but an exciting challenge. The need for it has been with us since the beginning of civilization. As the ancient Greek philosopher Aristotle explained in his *Nicomachean Ethics*:

> The virtues we get by first exercising them . . . so too we become just by doing just acts, temperate by doing temperate acts, brave by doing brave acts. . . . Hence also it is no easy task to be good . . . to do this to the right person, to the right extent, at the right time, with the right motive, and in the right way, that is not easy; wherefore goodness is both rare and laudable and noble. . . . It makes no small difference, then, whether we form habits of one kind or of another from our very youth; it makes a very great difference, or rather all the difference.[6]

This development of one's character is truly *The Ultimate Gift* that we hope to give to our young people. In the movie version of Jim Stovall's book of the same name, a privileged young man receives a most unexpected inheritance from his grandfather. Instead of the sizeable inheritance of cash that he expects, the young man receives 12 tasks—or "gifts"—designed to challenge him on a journey of self-discovery. The gifts confront him with character choices that force him to decide how one can be truly happy. Is it the possession of money that brings us happiness, or is it what we do with the money that we have? Every one of us has been given gifts. Will we keep our gifts to ourselves, or will we share them with others?

Being a "person of character" can have multiple meanings. Psychologist Steven Pinker asks an interesting question in a

January 13, 2008, *New York Times Magazine* article titled "The Moral Instinct": "Which of the following people would you say is the most admirable: Mother Teresa, Bill Gates or Norman Borlaug?" Pinker goes on to explain that although most people would say that, of course, Mother Teresa is the most admirable—a true person of character who ministered to the poor in Calcutta, was awarded the Noble Peace Prize, and was ranked in an American poll as the most admired person in the twentieth century—each of these three is a morally admirable person.

Pinker points out that Bill Gates made billions through his company Microsoft, but he also has decided to give away billions of dollars to help alleviate human misery in the United States and around the world. His charitable foundation is built on the principles that "All lives—no matter where they are being lived—have equal value" and "To whom much is given, much is expected."

Pinker notes that very few people have heard of Norman Borlaug, an agronomist who has spent his life developing high-yielding varieties of crops for third world countries. He is known as the "Father of the Green Revolution" because he used agricultural science to reduce world hunger and, by doing so, saved more than a billion lives. Borlaug is one of only five people in history to have won the Nobel Peace Prize, the Presidential Medal of Freedom, and the Congressional Gold Medal. He has devoted his long professional life and his scientific expertise to making the world a better place.

All of these people—although very different, from different places, and with different gifts—are people of character. They are, says Pinker, people with "a sixth sense, the moral sense." It is the sense of trying to do good in whatever situation one finds oneself.[7]

The authors and editors of the series *Character Education* hope that these books will help young readers discover their gifts and develop them, guided by a moral compass. "Do good and avoid evil." "Become all that you can be—a person of character." The books in this series teach these things and more. These books will correlate well with national social studies standards of learning. They will help teachers meet state standards for teaching social and emotional skills, as well as state guidelines for teaching ethics and character education.

Madonna M. Murphy, Ph.D.

Author of *Character Education in America's Blue Ribbon Schools* and professor of education, University of St. Francis, Joliet, Illinois

Sharon L. Banas, M.Ed.

Author of *Caring Messages for the School Year* and former character education coordinator and middle school social studies teacher, Sweet Home Central School District, Amherst and Tonawanda, New York

FOOTNOTES
1. William Kilpatrick. *Why Johnny Can't Tell Right from Wrong*, New York: Simon and Schuster, 1992.
2. Josephson Institute, 2006 *Josephson Institute Report Card on the Ethics of American Youth: Part One – Integrity.* Available online at: http://josephsoninstitute.org/pdf/ReportCard_press-release_2006-1013.pdf.
3. House Joint Resolution 366. May 11, 1994, 103rd Congress. 2d Session.
4. U.S. Army Center of Military History. *The Medal of Honor.* Available online at: www.history.army.mil/moh.html.
5. Thomas Lickona, *Educating for Character: Teaching Respect and Responsibility in the Schools.* New York: Bantam, 1991. Thomas Lickona, *Character Matters: How to Help Our Children Develop Good Judgment, Integrity, and Other Essential Virtues.* New York: Simon and Schuster Touchstone Books, 2004.
6. Richard McKeon, editor, "Nicomachean Ethics." *Basic Works of Aristotle,* Chicago: Random House, Clarendon Press, 1941.
7. Steven Pinker, "The Moral Instinct," *The New York Times,* January 13, 2008. Available online at www.newyorktimes.com.

WHAT IS TEAMWORK?

"Alone we can do so little; together we can do so much."

> —Helen Keller (1880–1968),
> author and activist for the blind and deaf

S ports players use it. Youth groups and scouting groups use it. School groups use it, and employers definitely use it. Behind virtually every big project is a team of people working together to get it done. The benefits of working with a team are spelled out right in the letters that make up the word: **T**ogether **E**veryone **A**chieves **M**ore. This simple idea of working together to accomplish more than any one person could do alone is the essence of teamwork.

Take, for example, the Millbrook High School 2006–2007 Junior Class Council of Raleigh, North Carolina. The council organized a school-wide effort to raise money for juvenile diabetes. Council members worked with leaders of the school's academic clubs and after-school groups to encourage them to participate in the fund-raiser. "Students made a meaningful personal connection to diabetes because several students in our school have it. We were all motivated to help our friends," explained class council president Eric Book. Together, the students raised more than $12,000. That is more than any other school in the entire state. By working together, everyone achieved more to help young people with diabetes.

The American Heritage Dictionary, Fourth Edition, defines teamwork as "the cooperative effort by the members of a group or team to achieve a common goal." At Millbrook High School, raising money for charity was the common goal. Each student contributed his or her own efforts toward reaching the goal. By cooperating with one another and individually committing themselves to the project, the students successfully accomplished the team's goal.

TEAM COMMITMENT

Imagine the best quarterback in the National Football League (NFL) standing alone on a football field. Without his teammates, or fellow members of his team, the player is just a person standing on a big patch of grass. Even the best player cannot win a game alone. Working with his team, however, the quarterback has the potential to win the Super Bowl.

Legendary football coach Vince Lombardi understood the importance of teamwork. As coach for the Green Bay Packers, Lombardi inspired his players and led his team to six division titles, five NFL championships, and two Super Bowls. Lombardi was such a successful coach that the Super Bowl trophy is named in his honor, the Vince Lombardi Trophy. According to Lombardi, the secret to teamwork is commitment: "Individual commitment to a group effort—that is what makes a team work, a company work, a society work, a civilization work." Lombardi committed to his team, and his team, in turn, committed to their coach. Offensive lineman Jerry Kramer said of Lombardi, "He made us all better than we thought we could be." Lombardi knew that commitment mattered on the field, but he also knew that it mattered in everyday life.

Most people will never play football in the NFL or have a coach like Vince Lombardi. Many will not even play sports at

Green Bay Packers coach Vince Lombardi, seen here getting a lift from his players after a 1960 victory, inspired his players to work successfully as a team to win games.

all. Almost everyone, however, will participate in a team at some point in his or her lives. Teamwork is the engine that powers our society. In the business world, teams brainstorm creative ideas, plan a company's future, and implement large projects. In nonprofit organizations, teams of volunteers run programs to better society. In the military, team members depend upon one another as they risk their safety in military operations. In athletics, teams compete to drive one another to greater levels of performance.

Each time a person joins a team, he or she faces a choice: commit to the team and its mission or not. That person's choice can be the difference between a successful team and a failing team. After all, no team ever won the Super Bowl without the commitment of every one of its players.

HOW TEAMS WORK

Teams come together in all sorts of ways. A team might be assigned to a school research project or selected for a sports event. A person might be hired to a team for an after-school job, or people might select their own teams for a science fair or service project. It does not matter whether teammates are great friends, if they have not gotten along in the past, or if they just met one another. What matters is that they learn to work together in a productive way.

Scholars Jon R. Katzenbach and Douglas K. Smith studied teamwork at some of the country's top companies. They

TEAM PRIDE

In 2004, nobody expected the incoming Naples High School freshman football team of Naples, Florida, to be very good. The players were not big enough. Their skills were not developed enough. According to the local newspaper, *The Naples Daily News,* even the players' own coach deemed the team "unremarkable."

That is until, as seniors, the Golden Eagles took home the 2007 Class 3A State Championship, capping off a perfect 15-0 season. Early in the game, the Naples High team faced fierce competition, but the players never gave up. They believed in one another and themselves. "It was all down to that, four years of work. . . . We did it when we had to," said player Kyle Lindquist.

The team's 17-10 victory thrilled hometown fans. "For all of Southwest Florida, we felt an obligation to make them proud," Coach Bill Kramer said. "Our guys gave every single bit that they had, and we were fortunate to come out on top."

Player Nick Alajajian knows that his team's win was due to the commitment and hard work of the entire team. "I'm so very proud of every one of my teammates. . . . Together we've got this 15-0 and a state championship," he said. With great pride, the formerly unremarkable team grew into remarkable champions of teamwork.

recorded common characteristics of successful teams. What they found provides clues to how the best teams work. In their 1993 *Harvard Business Review* article, "The Discipline of Teams," Katzenbach and Smith explained that members of the best teams "encourage listening and responding constructively to views expressed by others, giving others the benefit of the doubt, providing support, and recognizing the interests and achievements of others." Katzenbach and Smith also outlined three essential things that all teams need: a common purpose, goals, and diverse skills.

Teams need a common purpose. According to Katzenbach and Smith, teams work best when they have a common purpose, or reason for being on a team. The purpose may come from a leader, such as from a coach, teacher, or boss. For example, a science teacher might announce a school-wide competition to see which team can build a balsa wood bridge that supports the most weight. The students would have to come together to develop their bridge entries. The purpose may also come from within the team. For example, a group of friends might decide to create a service project to help support the military. Equipped with a common purpose, the team can focus on setting goals for itself.

Teams need goals. The only way to know if a team is succeeding in its purpose is for the team to set goals for itself. Goals are a way to check in with the work along the way. Katzenbach and Smith call these "specific and measurable performance goals." When a goal is specific, it is clear. Every member of the team understands what he or she is working toward. A measurable goal can be calculated. In other words, the team definitely knows whether or not it met its goal. For example, entering a bridge in the school competition is a common purpose. Building a bridge that supports more than 25 grams of weight is a specific and measurable goal. When the task is complete, either the bridge stands or it breaks under the weight. Likewise, beginning a service project for the military provides common purpose, but committing to send out 500 care packages to U.S. military personnel provides a goal that is specific and measurable for the team.

Teams need members with diverse skills. Finally, Katzenbach and Smith emphasize that the skills of team members are super important to a team's success. Teamwork is, after all, about dividing up the work. If every person on the bridge team has the skills to design the look of the bridge but no one has the skills to make it structurally sound, the team will have a difficult time with the project. Likewise, the service project will need a person to coordinate donations, one to focus on mailing, one to work with the military, etc. So, when bringing together teammates, it is important to think not just about team members' personalities but also about what skills each person brings to the team.

ISSUES SURROUNDING TEAMWORK

Teamwork is a learned skill, just like learning to swim or learning to solve an algebra problem. When a person is used to working alone, it may be a challenge to be part of a team. With commitment, however, any person can learn to become a team player. There are some common challenges to look out for to help the team be successful.

The first is accountability. Having a successful team depends on the entire team taking responsibility for the team's success. That means that every team member must do his or her part. When teammates feel that they can depend on one another, they develop trust. That is why it is important for team members to let their teammates know if they have been let down. When team members realize that their teammates depend on them, they are more likely to hold themselves accountable for the actions. When expressing disappointment to a teammate, a team member should keep in mind the goal of improving the relationship and strengthening the team, not causing more conflict and hurt feelings.

Another challenge to teamwork happens when the group is working really well together. Having a successful team is

TEAM INNOVATION

Every year, the Lemelson-MIT InvenTeams project provides grants to student teams around the country who work to develop a new invention to solve a problem. Teams must work together to identify a problem they wish to solve, research the problem, and then invent a prototype that solves the problem. Successfully inventing a new machine is not an easy task. In 2006, students from the John D. O'Bryant School of Mathematics and Science in Roxbury, Massachusetts, surveyed teachers

(continues)

As part of an InvenTeam project, students at John D. O'Bryant School of Mathematics and Science worked together to solve a problem at their school. They created an automatic portable blackboard eraser that can move horizontally across a blackboard.

(continued)

from their school about what kind of technology would help them. They found that chalkboard dust caused health problems for several of the teachers. The team set out to invent an automatic blackboard eraser, but they struggled to create a device that applied enough pressure to the board.

"It took a long time to make…a lot of trial and error. I learned a lot about teamwork and hard work," said team member Lidza Louina. The team's final product, the portable automatic blackboard eraser, or P.A.B.E., is proof of the team's success.

a great accomplishment. When a team becomes successful, it may find that there is less conflict within the group. When everyone on the team agrees all the time, a team may be starting to groupthink. Groupthink is when a group of people have the same ideas and no one challenges ideas. The danger of groupthink is that the team's ideas may be less creative or innovative. One way to avoid groupthink is to encourage team members to challenge ideas even if they agree with them. A team can always benefit from looking at ideas from all possible sides before making a decision.

Lastly, teamwork can be challenged by a lack of respect within the team. Team members must value one another as partners and respect each other's thoughts, ideas, and opinions. With respect, team members feel good about their team. Without it, the team will fall apart.

WHAT IS RESPECT?

2

"There is no respect for others without humility in one's self."

—*Henri Frédéric Amiel (1821–1881),*
Swiss philosopher and poet

I n 1967, the United States was in the midst of a cultural shift. The civil rights movement had made strides toward gaining equal rights for African Americans. Inspired by those successes, the women's movement was energized to fight for women's equality. That summer, Aretha Franklin released her own version of an Otis Redding song that would become an anthem for both movements. In the song, as its title suggests, Franklin demands one thing: "Respect."

The civil rights and women's movements were based on the idea that every person, regardless of race or gender, is worthy of respect. The same idea—that "all men are created equal"—is put forth in the Declaration of Independence, though at the time it was written that line meant white men (and not women, or men of other races). Throughout history, groups of people have courageously stood up to those in power in order to gain respect.

Respect is something that everyone wants and deserves, but people rarely stop to think about the meaning of the word. *The American Heritage Dictionary, Fourth Edition*, defines respect as "a feeling of appreciative, often deferential regard." To treat people with respect is to treat them as though they matter. In her book *What Do You Stand For?*, award-winning author and teacher Barbara A. Lewis explains that respect is "about *relationships*: with people we know and people we don't know; with our society, culture, government, and God or Higher Power; with the planet we live on and the living things we share with it; even with ourselves."

RESPECT IS A VIRTUE

Almost everyone has thought or heard someone say, "I want to be a good person." People have been trying to define what it means to be "good" since the beginning of civilization. The ancient Greek philosopher Aristotle wrote about the importance of virtues. Aristotle wrote that virtue is "concerned with choice . . . between two vices . . . with regard to what is best and right." In other words, a good, or virtuous, person chooses to do the right thing when faced with the choice between right and wrong. According to Aristotle, people gain some virtues though practice and habit. Wisdom is one example. If a person makes a habit of acting wisely, he or she will become a wise person.

In his 2004 book, *Character Matters*, author Thomas Lickona defines virtues as "objectively good human qualities." According to Lickona, a respected psychologist and educator, trends such as fashion and popular music may change, but virtues such as justice and kindness "transcend time and culture." Lickona means that being kind was "cool" in ancient Greece, it is cool today, and it will be cool in 100 years. Treating others with respect is cool, too. If a person makes a habit of acting with respect toward others, he or she will become a respectful person. A respectful person has one of the virtues that "good people" share.

SHOWING RESPECT MATTERS

The way people act provides clues about who they are. People who treat others with respect say with their actions, *I believe that every human being is important.* As Barbara A. Lewis writes, "When you treat all people with respect—especially those who can't do anything special for you—you accept what they are and appreciate what they *may become.* This type of respect is unselfish, sensitive, and the foundation for many other values and other character traits."

Showing respect to someone is not the same as having respect for that person. When a person *has* respect for someone, he or she is familiar with the person and admires him or her. A person may have respect for parents, a teacher, or a known leader. When a person *shows* respect, it does not matter if he or she knows or even likes the person. By showing respect to all people, we acknowledge that every person has the same right to life on Earth as every other person. The novelist Pearl S. Buck wrote in the book, *To My Daughters, With Love,* "You cannot make yourself feel something you do

A TEEN SHOWS RESPECT

During his eighth-grade year, Anthony Menard began volunteering at the Barton Senior Center in Barton, Vermont. Twice a week, he helped serve meals, pour coffee, make desserts, and wash dishes for the senior citizens at the center. Though he began volunteering to help others, Menard found that the experience positively impacted his own life. "The best part of volunteering with senior citizens is the knowledge and experience you gain from them," he said. Menard's community recognized his service work. Vermont Governor Jim Douglas awarded him the "Bridging the Generations" award for demonstrating respect for senior citizens. Anthony was also named "Outstanding Young Volunteer of the Year" by the Ladies Auxiliary to the Veterans of Foreign Wars.

not feel, but you can make yourself do right in spite of your feelings." When people show respect to others, even those they do not agree with or like, they show appreciation for the diversity that makes our planet interesting and special.

GETTING RESPECT

When people get respect, they feel good—both about themselves and about the person that respected them. Both the giver and the receiver of respect benefit. On the contrary, being disrespected makes people feel bad about themselves and others. Nobody benefits from disrespect. Comedian Rodney Dangerfield used to joke that he got "no respect." The character he created was always looking for respect, but he never found it. Because being respected feels good, many people look for ways to get respect from their peers, family, and strangers. Some people use bullying or rudeness to try to get it. Lewis explains why these methods do not work: "People *fear* bullies, but they don't *respect* them." In fact, the best way to be respected by others is simply to treat others with respect.

WAYS PEOPLE SHOW RESPECT

People communicate respect (or lack of it) with what they wear, say, and do. In his book *20 Things I Want My Kid to Know,* author and former high school teacher Hal Urban writes, "Showing our respect is the only proof that we have it." In other words, people only know we have respect when we show it to them.

With regard to respect, the old idiom, or expression, "actions speak louder than words" rings true. The things people do to show respect mean much more than simply saying they have it. Urban writes about four "pillars of respect," or actions that show respect: manners, language, honoring the rules, and appreciating differences. Two additional pillars could be added to Urban's list: clothing and following the Golden Rule.

Manners

Everyone can recall a time when he or she wasn't treated with respect or kindness. Most likely, the other person's rudeness made him or her feel upset, hurt, annoyed, or angry. In the early 1900s, Irish playwright George Bernard Shaw wrote, "Without good manners, human society becomes intolerable and impossible." He meant that nobody wants to live in a society of rude people. Being rude communicates a lack of consideration and respect for others. Being polite, on the other hand, communicates respect. Polite people have good manners. Given the choice between a society of rude people and a society of polite people, most people would choose polite.

Language

The language people use says a lot about them. Disrespectful people use disrespectful language. Disrespectful language focuses on the negative. It includes cursing, but it is more than that. Put-downs, sarcasm, complaints, pessimism, insults, lies, and rumors are all kinds of disrespectful language. Respectful language, on the other hand, focuses on the positive. It includes praise, encouragement, optimism, honesty, sympathy, thanks, and sincere compliments. Every year, high school teacher Hal Urban conducts a survey of language with the students in his class. Without fail, the students respond that they hear negative, disrespectful language more often than positive, respectful language. They even admit that they are more likely to speak negatively than positively. Urban encourages his students to focus on speaking more respectfully because "what comes out of our mouths does, indeed, reveal what's stored in our hearts." In other words, respectful language reveals a respectful person.

Clothing

Different styles of clothing are appropriate for different occasions. A person would obviously not wear a formal suit to the beach or a swimsuit to the prom. However, many people would not think twice about wearing jeans to a job interview. When people meet for the first time, clothing is one of the first things they notice. An employer interviewing a person in jeans might think, "This person does not respect me enough to dress for the interview. I'd rather hire someone else." Respectful people dress with the intent of making a good impression, no matter who they may meet.

Honoring the Rules

Parents have rules. Schools have rules. Sports have rules. Jobs have rules. Societies have rules (called laws). The reason for rules is so that every person lives by the same guidelines; or, as Urban writes, "to establish a sense of fairness." Sports provide a clear example of the necessity of rules—without them, there would be no games, no points, and no fairly chosen winners. Respectful people honor the rules because doing so respects the authority of the rule maker. Teens may not always like the rules their parents make, for example, but following those rules shows their parents respect. When parents feel their child respects them, they are more likely to respond by showing respect toward their child. They may even consider a change to the rules, if well presented. As adults, law-abiding citizens gain more respect in the community than criminals.

Appreciating Differences

In addition to diverse cultures, the world is full of people with diverse ideas. Each person has his or her own point of view about political issues, food, fashion, entertainment, etc. Sometimes, it is tempting to judge others because their ideas and preferences do not match our own. When people judge, according to Urban, they are saying, "You are not okay, because you are not like me." That is a self-centered and disrespectful way to think. If everyone shared the same viewpoint and ideas, the world would be pretty dull. There would not be new ideas for movies, artwork, novels, plays,

MAYA LIN RESPECTS VIETNAM VETERANS

In 1981, Maya Lin was a 21-year-old undergraduate student at Yale University. That year, Lin won a competition to design a memorial for the soldiers who died in the Vietnam War, a war fought from 1956 to 1975 between communist North Vietnam and its allies and U.S.-supported South Vietnam. Vietnam was an unpopular war, and many people still had bitter feelings about it. "The politics had eclipsed the veterans, their service, and their lives," Lin said.

Lin designed a simple and elegant memorial to honor the war's veterans. Carved into a wall of stone are the names of the 58,249 soldiers who gave their lives during the Vietnam War. At first, some people did not like the memorial because it looked different from traditional memorials. However, the Vietnam Veterans Memorial in Washington, D.C., has come to be one of America's most beloved monuments. It is a symbol of respect toward our country's military.

music, recipes, fashion, or political debate. There would not exist a richness of life that comes from different cultures. By appreciating the differences of others, we acknowledge that it is those differences that bring excitement and new ideas to the world.

FOLLOWING THE GOLDEN RULE

Everyone knows the Golden Rule: Treat others as you would like to be treated. Respectful people actually follow it. The Golden Rule is the foundation of showing respect to others. In fact, if people always treated others as they themselves wanted to be treated, there would be no need to mention the other pillars of respect. People would do them automatically. Living by the Golden Rule means paying attention to other people, showing them consideration, listening to them, learning about them, being kind, and lending a helping hand. When people live by the Golden Rule, they not only show others respect, but they also earn the respect of others. In addition, they demonstrate respect for themselves.

A MODEL OF RESPECT

As the wealthiest man in the world, Bill Gates, the cofounder of Microsoft, could have kept his billions of dollars for himself. Instead, Gates and his wife, Melinda, decided use their money to improve the lives of others. They started the Bill & Melinda Gates Foundation with one core philosophy: "We believe that all lives have equal value, no matter where they are being lived."

The foundation offers monetary grants to help solve important world problems, such as improving health and reducing extreme poverty in the developing world and improving education in the United States. The foundation has already committed to give more than $16 billion in grants to organizations such as the United Negro College Fund, Malaria Vaccine Initiative, Save the Children, and the United Way. By using their money to help all people lead healthy, productive lives, Bill and Melinda Gates demonstrate an incredible respect for humankind. Their work will make a lasting impact on the world.

ISSUES SURROUNDING RESPECT

It would be great if everybody showed respect all the time. Unfortunately, that is not the case. As Hal Urban points out, disrespectful language and behavior is common. It is not always easy to show respect, especially if one receives disrespect first. The good news is that every person has the opportunity to choose respect instead.

One issue surrounding respect pops up during disagreements. Without respect, a disagreement can quickly turn into an argument or fight. During the 2007 presidential primaries for the Democratic nomination, candidate Barack Obama said of his opponents, "We can disagree without

A GIFT OF RESPECT

In 2006, Warren Buffett, a stock market investor and the world's second-richest man, made an amazing announcement. He would give away 85 percent of his wealth to charity, most of it to the Bill & Melinda Gates Foundation. Over time, this foundation will receive $31 billion or more from Buffett, the largest gift ever given to such an organization.

Bill and Melinda Gates (*left and middle*) created their foundation with the belief that all lives are equally important. Above, they stand with Warren Buffett at a press conference in 2006 to announce Buffett's pledge to the foundation of 10 million Class B shares of his company, Berkshire Hathaway, which were valued at more than $31 billion.

Buffett was inspired by the generosity and hard work of the Gates, his friends. He had always planned to give away much of his wealth after his death. After seeing the Gates Foundation in action, however, he decided not to wait. "You don't get an opportunity like that ordinarily," he said. "I'm getting two people enormously successful at something, where I've had a chance to see what they've done, where I know they will keep doing it." Buffett shows great respect for the Gates and their mission.

In addition to his donation, Buffett joined the foundation to help Bill and Melinda distribute grants. The three work together as a team. Of their partnership with Buffett, the Gates said, "Working with Warren and with our partners around the world, we have a tremendous opportunity to make a positive difference in people's lives." That is a gift that benefits everyone.

being disagreeable." He meant that it is possible to disagree with someone's opinions and still show him or her respect. Showing respect to someone does not mean we have to agree with everything he or she says. If we did, we would not be respecting our own ability to make ideas, thoughts, opinions, and decisions. To disagree respectfully, a person should first listen to what the other person has to say. It is important to understand the other side. Then the person can voice his or her position and provide reasoning for it. If the two sides do not come to agreement, they may "agree to dis-agree." After all, everyone is entitled, or allowed, to have his or her own thoughts and opinions.

Most of the time people respond to respect with respect in return. Yet, it is not possible to control the behavior of oth-ers. Some people choose to be rude, mean, and disrespectful. When that happens, the disrespected person must assert his or her right to be treated with respect. One way to do that is to call attention to the disrespect. Teacher and author Bar-bara A. Lewis recommends speaking with the disrespectful person directly. Tell the person the specific words or behav-ior that disrespected you, how it affected you, and how you would like to resolve the issue. Perhaps the person did not realize the impact of his or her behavior and will agree to correct it. If the person continues to show disrespect, politely decline to continue your relationship. However, if the disre-spect becomes bullying or abuse, seek help from a counselor or another adult. Every person has the right to be treated with respect.

WHAT IS SELF-RESPECT?

"Whether you think you can, or you think you can't, you're right."

—Henry Ford (1863–1947), American automaker

It is nearly impossible to have respect for someone else until you have respect for yourself. That is because respect is about believing in the value of every human life. If you personally believe that all people matter, you must believe that you matter because you are a person. On the flip side, if you do not believe in the value of human beings, you will have a hard time believing in your own value. If you feel small, insignificant, like a loser or a jerk, too fat, too thin, not smart or fast enough, or if you beat yourself up in any other way, your thoughts and actions say that you don't respect yourself. If you don't respect yourself, it is very difficult to respect anyone else.

Earning respect from others also starts from within. It is easy to spot people with self-respect because they have something that people admire: confidence. Confident people look like they "feel comfortable in their own skin," stand tall, and speak their minds. Confident people stand out from the crowd simply by being themselves. People often naturally respect and admire confidence. On the other hand, when people lack confidence, they worry about what other people think of them or that their feelings and ideas are not important. They may try to blend in with everyone else or simply avoid contact with others. Their actions say, "I do not think I am good enough." Sometimes people without self-respect harm themselves. They take drugs and drink alcohol, skip school, or skip meals. They may think that these behaviors will make them feel good, look good, seem cool, or earn them respect, but they won't. The only way to earn respect is to have respect. That starts with taking care of oneself and having self-respect.

WAYS PEOPLE SHOW SELF-RESPECT

Self-respect is just like respect for others. The only way people prove they have it is by showing it. By practicing the basics of self-respect, people demonstrate a belief in their own self-worth. With commitment to the basics of self-respect, every person's self-confidence can grow. Other people will notice the difference, and you will too.

Speaking Up

One way to show self-respect is to speak up and say what's on your mind. The First Amendment to the U.S. Constitution guarantees the freedom of speech. That means that every person by law has the right to express his or her own thoughts, ideas, and opinions. This right is so important that it is one of the most basic principles of our government. We should not waste it by keeping our thoughts to ourselves. Speaking up is about recognizing that our opinions matter, even if others disagree. Imagine if Martin Luther King Jr. and other civil rights leaders had decided not to speak up about racism in the United States. The popular opinion at the time was that minorities did not deserve equal rights. Because brave people spoke up, they fought inequality and changed people's opinions and eventually laws. Our voices are our greatest powers for change.

MARJANE SATRAPI SPEAKS UP

Imagine growing up in a place where you could be killed just for talking negatively about the government. Marjane Satrapi experienced such a place—her native country of Iran—and even wrote a book and made a film about it. Satrapi grew up in Iran during the Islamic Revolution of the 1970s and 1980s. This revolution transformed Iran from a monarchy to an Islamic republic. At that time, a new government restricted the freedoms of Iranian people, especially women, but that did not stop Satrapi.

Marjane Satrapi was able to examine the realities of growing up during the Islamic Revolution in Iran by writing the graphic novel *Persepolis*, as well as codirecting an animated film based on the novel. Above, she attends a gala with the film's codirector, Vincent Parannaud, in New York City in 2008.

Satrapi's parents disagreed with the new government. They raised their daughter to think independently and question the world around her. While she did not always make the best decisions growing up (she dated guys who did not respect her, for example), Satrapi tried to learn from her mistakes. Eventually, she left Iran. She wrote the graphic novel *Persepolis* to share her experiences with the world. The book provides a glimpse of daily Iranian life rarely

(continues)

(continued)

seen before. It shows that people everywhere have hopes and dreams, even those living in restricted societies.

In 2007, Satrapi codirected an animated film based on her graphic novel. She had never made a film before but believed she could do it. The film was well received and was even nominated for a 2008 Academy Award for Best Animated Feature. "I realized I had talent I didn't know," said Satrapi. Satrapi's success demonstrates the importance of speaking up even when others try to stop you.

Admitting Mistakes

Another way to show self-respect is to admit mistakes. Everyone makes mistakes. It is a part of being human. Yet many people find it difficult to admit when they are wrong. In his book *Flawless! The Ten Most Common Character Flaws and What You Can Do About Them,* psychiatrist Louis Tartaglia says that the most common character flaw is "an addiction to being right." Being and doing right makes people feel good, so it is no surprise many people want to be right all the time. However, people who admit when they are wrong are honest with themselves and others. Being honest ultimately makes people feel better than winning an argument just for the sake of winning. When people admit mistakes and apologize for them, they not only show respect to those they wronged, but they also show respect to themselves.

Being Honest

People also show self-respect by being honest. In a 2008 article in *New York* magazine, journalist Po Bronson reviewed recent studies on teen honesty. According to the article, 98 percent of teenagers surveyed said that trust and honesty are essential in a personal relationship. Nearly the same percentage said that lying is morally wrong. That sounds like good news. However, when the same teens were asked about lying to their parents, 98 percent admitted that they had lied in the past. That means that almost all teenagers surveyed believe that lying is wrong and do it anyway. As Greek philosopher Aristotle explained, a virtuous person is one who knows the difference between right and wrong and chooses right.

Helping Others

Self-respect also comes from helping others. A 2005 study by the Corporation for National and Community Service and the U.S. Census Bureau found that 55 percent of American teenagers had volunteered in the previous year, nearly double the rate of adults. Volunteers in the study reported that volunteering improved their lives. The study found that young people who volunteer are more likely to believe they can make a positive impact in their community, to take an interest in current events, and to talk about politics with friends and parents. In addition, young people who volunteer do better in school than those who do not volunteer. When people help others by volunteering, they feel good about themselves and it shows.

Attending School

Having self-respect is also about working hard to succeed. Most young people know that better education leads to more job opportunities and higher income later in life, but they may not know that staying in school may actually help them live longer. According a 2007 article in *The New York Times,* study after study finds that educated people live longer, healthier lives than uneducated people or those who drop out of school.

Taking Care of Yourself

People who respect themselves respect their bodies. They eat right, exercise, get enough sleep, and floss and brush their

Volunteering has a positive impact on the volunteer's life, as well as on the people and places the volunteer is helping. Above, Donnie Ferrell, a volunteer teacher's aide, helps fifth-grader Gary Jensen do his work at Havasupai Elementary School in Lake Havasu City, Arizona, in 2005.

teeth. They maintain a healthy body image and do not fall prey to media images that tell them to look a certain way. They draw the line when people try to pressure them sexually. It is not always easy. From fast-food commercials to rail-thin models on magazines covers to teen pregnancy comedy movies, the messages sent to young people about how to treat their bodies are completely mixed up. The best advice is to ignore the media, and treat your body right. By respecting your body, you respect yourself.

Avoiding Alcohol, Cigarettes, and Drugs

References to smoking, drugs, and alcohol are everywhere in pop culture. Celebrities are often more famous for trips to rehab than for the movies and music they produce. A recent study by the University of Pittsburgh School of Medicine found that one-third of the 279 top songs of 2005 had explicit references to substance abuse. Of these, two-thirds portrayed drugs, alcohol, and smoking in a positive light. The 2008 Grammy winner for Best Song was "Rehab" by Amy Winehouse (lyrics include: "They tried to make me go to rehab, I said no, no, no . . ."). The singer-songwriter wrote the song about her own experiences of not wanting to go to rehab for her drug and alcohol addictions. Some critics argued that it was wrong for her to win such a prestigious award for that song. They pointed out that her continued drug use was well-documented at the time of the ceremony and awarding that sort of behavior gives off a bad message.

According to a 2005 study by the National Center for Education Statistics, 16 percent of all high school seniors reported smoking cigarettes daily, 29 percent reported binge drinking (5 or more drinks) in the previous two weeks, and 23 percent used illicit drugs (marijuana, cocaine, heroin, hallucinogens, amphetamines, or abuse of prescription drugs) in the previous 30 days. A 2005 study called "Monitoring the Future" found that 75 percent of twelfth-graders had tried alcohol. At some point, every young person will face the choice of whether or not to light his or her first cigarette, take his or her first drink, or try drugs for the first time. Contrary to some media images, all of these substances harm the body (in short- and long-term ways) and impair the mind. According to the Centers for Disease Control and Prevention, young people who drink alcohol are more likely to have problems at school and have unwanted, unplanned, or unprotected sexual activity. Plus, they are at a higher risk for alcohol-related car crashes and other injuries and at a higher risk for suicide and homicide. In addition, youths who start drinking before age 15 are five times more likely to develop alcohol dependence or abuse later in life than those who begin drinking after age 21. For preteens and teens with a healthy dose of self-respect, the choice is clear: smoking, drugs, and alcohol are not for them.

Stopping Self-Destruction

Self-destruction is when a person willingly engages in behaviors that he or she knows will harm him- or herself. Sometimes, when people have little or no self-worth, they want to harm themselves. Self-destruction can appear in many forms—reckless driving, smoking, drugs and alcohol, cutting oneself, eating disorders, or any number of other behaviors. A person who is self-destructive needs help. If you or someone you know is harming him or herself, speak to a trusted adult, such as a teacher, guidance counselor, or coach.

Setting and Achieving Goals

Having self-respect and self-worth is about believing in one's own abilities. When people set goals for themselves and achieve them, they feel a sense of pride in their accomplishments. They feel good about themselves. Goals can be simple and short-term, such as getting an A on an upcoming history test, or complex and long-term, such as earning a history degree from a university. Goals give people a sense of purpose and a way to focus on the future. Setting and achieving goals is a great way to build and maintain self-respect.

Applying the Golden Rule to One's Self

Often, people follow the Golden Rule and treat others as they want to be treated, but they do not offer themselves the same respect. All people have an inner voice that sometimes serves as a reminder about the things we don't like about ourselves. When people think badly of themselves or disrespect their bodies, they violate the Golden Rule. Sometimes it is easy to see when someone else is rude, mean, or treats us poorly, but it is difficult to identify when we do it to ourselves. The next time your inner voice tells you that you are not good enough, ask yourself, "Would I say these things to someone else?" If the answer is no, try thinking about your talents and the good things that you do instead of comparing yourself to others.

ISSUES SURROUNDING SELF-RESPECT

People make choices every day that affect their self-respect. When people are proud of their choices, they gain self-respect. When they are disappointed in their choices, they lose self-respect. A conscience is the voice inside each person that weighs whether he or she is proud or disappointed. According to Thomas Lickona, conscience is very important. In his

RESPECT YOUR RIGHTS

Courtney Macavinta and Andrea Vander Pluym, authors of the book *Respect: A Girl's Guide to Getting Respect & Dealing When Your Line Is Crossed*, outline a list of rights that all people, male and female, share. As they point out, you have a RIGHT to:

* Feel like you belong and are an equal
* Figure out what you need and take care of yourself
* Listen to your true feelings
* Speak your mind, change your mind, and question the world around you
* Be different from your family, your friends, and media ideals and images
* Feel and be safe
* Follow your passions and be the real you

book *Educating for Character,* Lickona says that people with a developed conscience feel guilt when they do not live up to their own standards of how to act. They promise themselves to do better next time. When people do not have a developed conscience, they do not feel the need to adjust their behavior when they do things that are wrong. There are many different events that happen constantly to force people to face their conscience and challenge them to earn self-respect.

Self-Esteem

Sometimes people make choices that harm themselves because they have low self-esteem, or feel badly about themselves. Their decisions can cause them to lose self-respect. However, having high self-esteem alone does not equal having self-respect. Some people boost their self-esteem by buying expensive things, for example. According to Lickona, people with healthy self-esteem get it by having values such as honesty, kindness, and responsibility and not by having superficial ideals such as money, clothing, and popularity.

In the book *The 7 Habits of Highly Effective Teens*, author Sean Covey writes about two habits that he calls "the tumor twins," because they "slowly eat you away from the inside." These self-esteem-damaging habits are competition and comparing one's self to others. According to Covey, competition is healthy when people compete against their own personal best, but it is unhealthy when they use it to place themselves above another person. Like competition, comparing yourself to others, in Covey's words, is "nothing but bad news." That is because each person is different, each develops differently, and each has different skills. When we base our self-esteem on how we measure up to others, we will feel good about ourselves only when we feel superior to everyone else. When someone comes along who is better than us at something, our self-esteem will take a nosedive. Eliminating the two bad habits of competition and comparing from our lives will help each person develop healthy self-esteem and respect.

Pressure

Pressure is another issue surrounding self-respect. Young people face pressure from all kinds of sources—from friends, family, teachers, and coaches; from advertisements and media images; and even from themselves. We hear all the time about peer pressure to do drugs and alcohol, but pressure can be more subtle and difficult to ignore. For example, parents might pressure their child to join the soccer team when he or she really would rather join the band. In their book *Respect*, authors Courtney Macavinta and Andrea Vander Pluym encourage young people to listen to their "gut" in the face of pressure. According to the authors, the "gut" is the little voice inside that tells each person how he or she really feels about something. They point out that lots of people ignore their true feelings because they want to please others, they are afraid of looking bad, or they think it will be easier to do what is more popular or accepted. However, when people go against their instincts, they end up doing things they wish they had not done. By listening to their true feelings, people take control of their own choices and show themselves the respect they deserve. Ultimately, others will respect their integrity, or commitment to acting according to moral values.

Being Humble

Sometimes people equate having self-respect with gloating or feeling superior, but they are not related. In her famous 1968 essay "On Self-Respect," journalist Joan Didion writes that self-respect "has nothing to do with the approval of others." In other words, a person cannot gain self-respect by winning over other people or convincing others of his or her worth. By the same measure, a person cannot get self-respect by make others feel inferior so that he or she may feel superior. People who truly have self-respect remain humble about

A TEEN TAKES A STAND

Ava Lowery believes she has the power to end the war in Iraq—or she at least plans to try. In 2005, the Alabama teenager started the Web site PeaceTakesCourage.com to speak out against the war. Lowery makes short viral videos that are passed on through emails and blogs. The videos show people of the war's toll on soldiers and civilians.

Speaking out against the war has come with a tough price. Lowery has received hate mail and death threats from people who disagree with her views. She considered shutting down the site, but, she said, "I realized that if I shut my Web site down because of death threats, I would just be proving that they could shut me down."

Teenager Ava Lowery took a stand when she started her Web site to speak out against the war in Iraq. In this image, she stands with peace activist Cindy Sheehan in Montgomery, Alabama, in 2007, during Sheehan's "Summer of Love '07" walk.

Lowery's videos have received national attention. She has been featured by CNN, *The New York Times*, and other news organizations. The National Organization for Women (NOW) awarded her the 2007 Woman of Action Award. Lowery is happy for the attention but hopes that people look past her age and "focus on my message of peace."

their successes. They have no need to brag or boast about themselves because they do not need to convince anyone of their value. People looking to others for respect may talk themselves up or try to knock others down, but, as Didion notes, they will never find self-respect that way. People with self-respect will ignore those that try to make them feel inferior because they realize it is the others, and not them, who need self-respect.

Standing Up

Sometimes acting with self-respect means making tough choices, standing up for what one knows is right rather than what is easy or expected. For example, a person may decide to betray a friend's trust in order to report that his or her friend is being abused. By making that choice, the person risks losing a friendship; however, he or she may also save the friend's life.

Taking a stand can also mean expressing a viewpoint that is unpopular. For example, a student may take issue with having a separate line for free lunches at the school cafeteria. He or she may gather a petition with other students to persuade the school to change the line system so that students who receive free lunches do not feel embarrassed to receive their meal. People with self-respect believe in their ability to act for the good—they understand that sometimes the tough choice is the right choice. It takes courage to trust your voice and to stand up for what is right, especially when others would rather you back down.

Forgiving One's Own Mistakes

Poet Maya Angelou once said in an interview, "I don't know if I continue, even today, always liking myself. But what I learned to do many years ago was to forgive myself. It is very important for every human being to forgive herself or himself because if you live, you will make mistakes." Just as we should apologize to others when we wrong them, we should apologize to ourselves when we wrong ourselves. Just as a gracious person will accept our apology and move forward, so should we. There is grace in forgiveness and vowing to try to do better next time. When we accept ourselves as human beings who make mistakes, we find self-respect.

THE VIRTUES OF TEAMWORK

"What you do not want done to yourself, do not do to others."

—*Confucius (551–479 B.C.),*
ancient Chinese philosopher

An ancient Chinese proverb says, "Acquiring virtue is better than acquiring gold." Like money, virtue is something that human beings must earn. Unlike money, there is no way to win the virtue lottery. At times, earning virtue can be difficult. It is often easier to ignore what is right and do what you want rather than think about how each action might turn out or make someone feel. Greek philosopher Aristotle once wrote, "It is easy to perform a good action, but not easy to acquire a settled habit of performing such actions." Becoming a virtuous person requires a commitment to performing good actions. When people make a habit of virtuous actions, the rewards to themselves and others are "better than acquiring gold." In other words: Being good pays off.

Working on a team provides an opportunity to practice many of life's virtues. Teams are like mini-versions of the world at large. They encourage relationships among people who may not have otherwise come together. Sometimes it may seem easier to look out for number one and try to perform solo, but it pays off to work well on a team. The payoff can be building friendships with teammates, accomplishing a big task, or succeeding as a group. The success or failure of a team relies on all team members making a commitment to practice the virtues of teamwork.

VIRTUES AND EFFECTIVE TEAMWORK

It may be tempting to think of a team as a machine. In a machine, each part has a specific task to do in order to function properly. While team members do have roles, a team is more like a family than a machine. Team members, like family members, must interact with one another in order to get things done. Because team members are human, they bring their emotions with them into the team. Just like in a family, without an emotionally supportive environment, a team becomes dysfunctional. In their article "Building the Emotional Intelligence of Groups," scholars Vanessa Urch Druskat and Steven B. Wolff state that effective teams are those with high "emotional intelligence," or consideration of the team's state of mind.

Emotional intelligence is measured by an emotional intelligence quotient (EQ), which is like an IQ for emotions. In the best-selling 1995 book *Emotional Intelligence,* author and psychologist Daniel Goleman describes an experiment done with four-year-olds at Stanford University in California. Researchers brought the children into a room that contained a table. On the table was a big, fluffy marshmallow. The kids were left alone in the room and told they could have the one marshmallow now or they could wait for the researcher to return and have two marshmallows. Some kids couldn't wait and grabbed the marshmallow right away, while others waited patiently for their sweet reward. Fast-forward 14 years to when the same kids were graduating from high school. The kids who showed self-control and waited were more popular with their peers and scored higher on achievement tests than those who had grabbed the marshmallows. The experiment showed that being smart about emotions, such as controlling impulses, is just as important for success as having brain power. People who develop their emotional intelligence and not just their smarts (or IQ) have a better chance for success. By practicing the following virtues, teams can build their emotional intelligence and work more effectively.

Caring

One can clearly see the difference between a plant that has been cared for and one that has not. The tended plant thrives and grows, while the neglected one withers away. The same is true of people. Caring is about giving your attention and

TEAM BUILDING

Scholars Vanessa Urch Druskat and Steven B. Wolff recommend following these rules to build the emotional intelligence of teams:

1. Take time away from group tasks to get to know one another.
2. Tell your teammates what you think and how you are feeling.
3. Ask whether everyone agrees with a decision.
4. Ask quiet members what they think.
5. Set ground rules and use them to point out poor behavior.
6. Validate all contributions. Let members know they are valued.
7. Respect individuality and differences in perspectives. Listen.
8. Never be derogatory or demeaning.
9. Assume that poor behavior happens for a reason. Find out what the reason is without being negative.
10. Emphasize that the team can meet the challenge. Be optimistic.

time. On a team, a caring person looks out for teammates as well as for him- or herself.

Loyalty

In his 1995 book *My American Journey*, former secretary of state Colin Powell addresses loyalty: "When we are debating an issue, loyalty means giving me your honest opinion, whether you think I'll like it or not. Disagreement, at this stage, stimulates me. But once a decision has been made, the debate ends. From that point on, loyalty means executing the decision as if it were your own." Loyalty is about sticking with your teammates and respecting the team's decisions. It is about committing to one another.

Empathy

When a person has empathy, he or she sees things from another person's perspective. Empathy is a deep understanding of another's feelings. It is seeing where someone is coming from. Empathy is very useful on teams because it helps teammates understand one another.

Honesty

When teammates are honest with one another, they build trust and commitment to the project. According to scholars Jon R. Katzenbach and Douglas K. Smith, who studied teamwork at some of the country's top companies, teams that are bonded by commitment hold themselves accountable for the success of the team. Everyone works harder to accomplish the team's goals.

Fairness

Each person carries equal weight. Each person's ideas are heard equally. Each person makes an important contribution. That is the essence of fairness. A team that is fair does not take advantage of anyone and gives each person equal opportunity to shine.

RESPECT IN TEAMWORK

A team's most important virtue is respect. With it, teammates work together as a unit. Without it, teammates work against one another. Teammates who respect one another and themselves are more likely to work hard to help the team reach its goals. The reason is that respect breeds motivation. Disrespect, on the other hand, kills it. If your friend insults your clothing, for example, you probably would not want to go shopping with him or her. However, if he or she appreciates your style and genuinely wants your help choosing outfits, you probably would give up your other plans to spend the whole day at the mall with him or her. Teams work the same way.

Members of the Screen Actors Guild teamed up with striking TV and movie writers to protest in support of a better contract for Writers Guild of America members in 2007. Above, actress Julia Louis-Dreyfus (*center, in cap*) joins striking writers in Los Angeles.

There is a feeling of cooperation, collaboration, and friendship on teams that demonstrates respect. In fact, all of the virtues of teamwork are tied to giving and receiving respect.

Respectful team members show up on time to team meetings because they know the team's time together is valuable. They are dependable. They listen openly when their teammates speak. They consider all of the ideas put forth, not just the ones that match their own. When respectful team members speak, they try to communicate their ideas clearly and make sure everyone understands them correctly. They use positive, optimistic language. They make an effort to include everyone and make sure every team member has an important job to do. Respectful team members do not hesitate to help a teammate. They are willing to go above and beyond to help the team succeed. When a fellow teammate does a good job, respectful teammates celebrate the accomplishment. They don't get jealous or resentful because they know that the success of the team depends on every team member's success. When an entire team is respectful, it is bound to succeed.

SELF-RESPECT IN TEAMWORK

Equally important for a team is self-respect. Perhaps you have heard the expression, "There is no 'I' in *team*." While it is true that individuals on a team sacrifice their personal needs for the team's needs, no team member should fade into the background. Each person has something valuable to contribute. Having self-respect encourages individuals to step up and make their contribution to the team.

When teammates demonstrate self-respect, they put their best foot forward. They express their honest ideas and opinions because they know that their ideas matter. That being said, they also know that their ideas are not the only ideas that matter. Therefore, team members with self-respect resist the urge to be self-centered. They realize that sometimes it is better to let go of a personal opinion for the good of the

A CHEATER HURTS HER TEAM

In 2000, Marion Jones was dubbed the fastest woman on Earth. In Sydney, Australia, Jones became the first woman to win five medals in a single Olympics: gold in the 100-, 200-, and 4x400-meter relays; bronze in the long jump and 4x100-meter relay. Eight years later, she had lost it all. Jones revealed that she had taken performance-enhancing drugs (steroids) and lied about it. The International Olympic Committee (IOC) stripped Jones of her medals. She was later sentenced to six months in prison for lying to investigators.

(continues)

When it was discovered that Marion Jones (*right*) used steroids during the 2000 Summer Olympics in Sydney, Australia, she was disqualified and asked to return her medals. Seven years later, her teammates (*from left:* Jearl Miles-Clark, Monique Hennagan, and LaTasha Colander-Richardson) were told they would have to give up their medals, too, since their teammate broke the rules. Here, the teammates proudly display their gold medals after winning the women's 4x400 meter relay.

(continued)

Jones's choices affected her relay teammates, too. In April 2008, the IOC executive board disqualified and stripped the medals from Jones's eight teammates. "The decision was based on the fact that they were part of a team, that Marion Jones was disqualified from the Sydney Games due to her own admission that she was doping during those games," IOC spokeswoman Giselle Davies said. "She was part of a team and she competed with them in the finals." Jones's teammates are refusing to return their medals and have hired a lawyer to defend their case.

Jones expressed regret for her actions. "I truly hope that people will learn from my mistakes," she said. Yet, because Marion Jones decided to cheat, her teammates may lose their Olympic glory.

team. Self-respecting team members contribute their best efforts to the team's work. They are proud of the work that they do. When the team's task is complete, team members that perform their best feel good about themselves and the job they did. Their pride in their work earns them even more self-respect.

SITUATIONS THAT TEST TEAMWORK

A rival team accidentally leaves their project plans out for anyone to see. Would you sneak a peek? You do not get along with your teammates at all. Would you quit the team? One particular team member is a total slacker. Would you give him the boot? There are plenty of situations that test teamwork. Think of them as opportunities to show off your problem-solving skills.

Cheating

In his book, *Educating for Character*, author and educator Thomas Lickona describes a survey he conducted about academic honesty. In the survey more, than 90 percent of college students responded that they believe it is wrong to cheat on a test, copy another student's assignment, submit another's paper as one's own, or copy word for word from a book without crediting the author. However, when the students were asked if they would do these things if they knew they would not be caught, nearly half the students answered "yes." In another study by Rutgers University, 76 percent of business students admitted to cheating on a test. A study by the Pinnacle Group in Minnesota found that 59 percent of high school students surveyed would willingly face six months of probation to do a business deal worth $10 million, and 67 percent said they would lie to achieve a business objective.

Cheating is common beyond the classroom, too. In 2002, Enron and WorldCom were exposed as corrupt companies that robbed investors of tens of millions of dollars. In 2007, the U.S. Senate's *Mitchell Report* revealed widespread use of steroids and HGH (human growth hormone) in Major League Baseball. Other professional sports organizations have faced doping scandals as well.

Deciding whether to cheat is a moral dilemma. The pressure to succeed or the opportunity to make a buck might make cheating seem reasonable. The problem with cheating is that it eliminates the possibility of fairness. If one team has an advantage, another team is at a disadvantage. If executives at Enron line their pockets with investors' dollars, hardworking people lose their retirement savings. Baseball players that cheat defraud the fans of the opportunity to see genuine athletes compete. Regardless of the possibility of getting caught, a team that respects itself does not cheat.

Conflict

Any time individuals with different backgrounds, ideas, and beliefs come together on a team, they will not always agree or get along. Yet it is this kind of diversity that enriches, or

Conflict between teammates is normal, but compromise is essential to resolving any disagreement. Above, Russian defender Sergei Ignashevich (*left*) and Russian goalkeeper Igor Akinfeev argue during the European Championship quarter-final football match against the Netherlands in 2008.

adds value, to the team's experience by bringing together people with unique skills and points of view. Many people would prefer to avoid conflict altogether, but often, conflict and debate bring teams to the most creative ideas. By listening openly to one another, teammates may be able to find a compromise that works for everyone.

Slackers

A slacker is a person who does not do a fair share of the work and is not invested in the team's success. Think about a game of tug-of-war. If one or two people are not pulling on the rope, the rope will become slack. The others must "pick up the slack" or else concede the game. Slackers bring negative feelings into the group because other team members feel they have to pick up the slack and do extra work. Rather than blowing up at a slacker or talking behind his or her back, it is best to make an effort to find out why that person is not performing. Maybe he or she is overscheduled, or has problems at home. Maybe the person doesn't even realize he or she isn't doing a fair share of the work. According to Druskat and Wolff, it is best to approach a slacker with an open mind and a sense of humor. The goal is to let the team member know that he or she is an important member of the team and that you need him or her help for the team to succeed.

TEAMWORK IN HISTORY

"We must all hang together, or assuredly we shall all hang separately."

—Benjamin Franklin (1706–1790),
American inventor and statesman

I n the summer of 1776, members of the Continental Congress gathered together to declare the American colonies' independence from Great Britain. Signing the Declaration of Independence was an act of rebellion that would surely lead to war. It had taken months of careful planning to reach agreement over the document. As the signers gathered to make the declaration official, Ben Franklin joked about sticking together through the struggle they would face as a result of the document. He knew that writing his name on the document meant becoming a traitor in the eyes of the British government. Unless the leaders of the colonies remained united, they would certainly face death in defeat.

The founders of the United States built our country by using teamwork. When the first colonists sailed to the east coast of North America in the 1600s, it took teamwork to build homes and establish communities. Later, when those colonists protested British rule, it was teamwork that allowed them to declare their independence. And again, the scrappy, ill-equipped Continental Army used teamwork (and a bit of

Teamwork was key in creating the Declaration of Independence for colonial America. In this image, Benjamin Franklin, Thomas Jefferson, John Adams, Robert Livingston, and Roger Sherman are seen working together to draft the document in 1776.

help from the French) to defeat the mighty British Army. Time and time again throughout our nation's history, teamwork has shone through as the crucial element of our successes.

DECLARING INDEPENDENCE

"We have it in our power to begin the world again." These words, written by Thomas Paine in January 1776, helped move forward the cause of American independence. Before

A CONSTITUTIONAL COMPROMISE

More than 10 years after the Declaration of Independence, Benjamin Franklin was part of another team that changed the course of American history. The fledgling country had endured a terrible war to gain its independence. It had established a weak government that gave most of the power to the states. If the United States was to survive, it needed a stronger government. On May 25, 1787, Franklin joined delegates from each of the states (except Rhode Island) to make a new plan of government. This meeting came to be called the Constitutional Convention.

The delegates at the convention faced a difficult challenge: creating a strong central government that did not diminish the power of the states. James Madison of Virginia introduced the Virginia Plan, which divided states' power by population. Madison's plan favored largely populated states, such as Virginia. William Patterson of New Jersey countered with the New Jersey Plan, which gave each state equal power regardless of population. Patterson's plan favored smaller states such as New Jersey. For more than a month, the sides debated the plans. Finally, Roger Sherman of Connecticut proposed the Great Compromise, a plan that created the Senate and House of Representatives as we know them today. The disagreements about the Constitution did not end there, however. Delegates also disagreed about slavery and systems of voting. Finally, on September 17, 1787, all 39 delegates signed the Constitution. It had taken four months of teamwork to reach an agreement.

Paine published his famous *Common Sense* pamphlet, the colonies were deeply divided about independence. Paine's clear and compelling words persuaded many people to join his cause. As Paine indicated, it would take teamwork and the power of "we" to achieve it.

In June of 1776, the Continental Congress brought together a committee of five men to write the first draft of the Declaration of Independence. They were John Adams of Massachusetts, Benjamin Franklin of Pennsylvania, Robert Livingston of New York, Roger Sherman of New Jersey, and Thomas Jefferson of Virginia. Each member contributed ideas to the document, but it was Jefferson who wrote the now famous words. After two weeks of writing, Jefferson brought his work to Franklin and Adams, who made some changes to the document. They then brought the declaration before the Congress.

Members of Congress debated Jefferson's words for two days. They questioned Jefferson's choice to harshly criticize King George. They also worried that southern colonies would reject Jefferson's condemnation of slavery. In the end, the committee compromised and removed much of the controversial language. On July 4, 1776, the Continental Congress approved the Declaration of Independence. Signing this document was the first step toward American independence.

DANIEL BOONE AND WILDERNESS ROAD

While politicians and statesmen debated the merits of independence, explorers and pioneers settled lands west of the Appalachians. On June 7, 1769, explorer Daniel Boone and trader John Findley set foot on the lands that would become Kentucky. The two men had found a natural path through the Appalachian Mountains from North Carolina that they called the Cumberland Gap. Sensing an opportunity to make a profit, the Transylvania Company of North Carolina purchased large portions of what would become Kentucky and Tennessee from the Cherokee Indians who inhabited the

In 1775, Daniel Boone hired a hardworking team of 30 woodsmen to help him create a path that would become Wilderness Road, a trail for Americans traveling west. In this painting, Boone and his wife Rebecca are shown taking settlers westward to Kentucky.

area. In 1775, the company hired Boone to build a passage through the Cumberland Gap.

Boone hired 30 woodsmen to forge usable trails through the Cumberland Gap to the west. The men worked tirelessly together to clear a path through the overgrown mountain wilderness. The path had to be large enough to accommodate traveling groups of men, women, and children. The completed route came to be called Wilderness Road. Just a few months after its completion, Daniel Boone and his family traveled Wilderness Road and established a settlement called Boonesborough, Kentucky. Soon other pioneers followed. It had taken months of hard work, but it was worth it. Wilderness Road became the primary route for Americans headed west.

THE CORPS OF DISCOVERY

In 1803, the United States purchased the Louisiana Territory from France and roughly doubled the size of our country. The territory was so large that some people were unsure of what it contained. President Thomas Jefferson, who years earlier had written the Declaration of Independence, hired Meriwether Lewis to lead an expedition into the territory. He instructed Lewis to follow the Missouri River, looking for a passage to the Pacific Ocean to "take careful observations of latitude and longitude at all remarkable points on the river."

Lewis asked William Clark to join him in leading the expedition. Together, the explorers set out to build a team of "good hunters, stout, healthy, unmarried men, accustomed to the woods, and capable of bearing bodily fatigue in pretty considerable degree." Clark also brought along an enslaved African named York. Together, the 33-member group, specially selected for their skills, became known as the Corps of Discovery.

In May 1804, the Corps of Discovery set out from St. Charles, Missouri, heading upstream on the Missouri River. Although much of the land had been unexplored by Europeans, Native American groups had lived there for a long time. One part of Lewis and Clark's mission was to establish relationships with native groups. In 1805, a Shoshone Indian woman named Sacagawea joined the group to help with this mission. Along with her husband, Sacagawea served as an interpreter and guide, helping navigate Indian trails all the way to the Pacific Ocean.

In 1806, the Corps of Discovery returned to St. Louis, Missouri, its mission accomplished. Together, they had traveled more than 8,000 miles (12,875 km). Lewis wrote praise of his team to the U.S. government, "The ample support they

gave me under every difficulty . . . the patience and fortitude . . . entitles them to my warmest . . . thanks."

THE TRANSCONTINENTAL RAILROAD

By the mid-1800s, thousands of people had made the overland passage from St. Louis to the westernmost United
States. Some had gone to start new lives on the western
frontier. Others went searching for gold. Still others went to
find a place to practice their religion outside of mainstream
society. Travel in horse-drawn covered wagons was difficult
and dangerous. In 1862, President Abraham Lincoln signed
the Pacific Railway Act, authorizing the construction of a
transcontinental railway.

Two rail companies worked to build the railroad line.
Central Pacific began in Sacramento, California, and moved
east. Union Pacific began in Omaha, Nebraska, and moved
west. They would meet in Promonontory Summit, Utah. The
rail companies brought in thousands of Chinese immigrants
to complete the dangerous railroad construction—blasting
tunnels though mountains, laying track, and driving rail
spikes. Workers faced deadly attacks from Native American
groups who sought to drive the railroad companies away. On
April 28, 1869, workers from Central Pacific astonished the
world by laying 10 miles of rail in a single day. Finally, on
May 10, the transcontinental railroad was complete. Telegraphs
transmitted the sound of the final spike being driven into the
ground from coast to coast. On both coasts, canons fired shots
into the ocean as a signal to the world that the railroad was
complete. Now transportation between New York and San
Francisco would take just one week. Our nation had become
more connected, and the world would never be the same.

THE PANAMA CANAL

By the late 1800s, the transcontinental railroad had helped
ease overland travel across the United States, but ocean
travel was still tricky. To get from the Atlantic Ocean to the

Pacific Ocean required sailing all the way around South America. A trip from New York to San Francisco by boat took months. As trade between east and west and Europe and the Americas increased, so did the need for a more direct route to the Pacific Ocean.

In 1881, the French began work on a canal through the Isthmus of Panama, which would allow boats to pass right through Central America. First they spent months clearing the jungle land. Then they began digging into the earth.

A crew of 150 men learned the importance of teamwork while creating the Panama Canal in Culebra, Panama. Part of their job involved lifting and shifting train tracks by hand.

However, the French did not realize the rainy season was about to hit. Workers spent day after day digging in chest-deep mud only to have their work washed away by torrential rains. Disease-carrying mosquitoes bred in pools of fresh-water. Thousands of workers died from malaria, smallpox, and yellow fever while making very little progress on the canal. Soon the French were ready to abandon the project.

Then in 1902, U.S. president Theodore Roosevelt bought the rights to the canal from the French. "No single great material work . . . is as of such consequence to the American people," he said. At first, the Americans had no better luck than the French. But then a new leader took over. He instructed workers to stop digging and start cleaning. By sanitizing the area, workers were able to get rid of much of

TWO DREAMERS LOOK TO THE SKY

In the early 1900s, two brothers dreamed of flight. Wilbur and Orville Wright were determined to put a man in the skies. Together they researched all the available information about aviation. Then they conducted experiments with kites, gliders, and a wind tunnel. Armed with the knowledge of these experiments, Wilbur and Orville designed and built an airplane. On December 14, 1903, the two brothers tested their invention. They flipped a coin to determine who would be the first pilot. Wilbur won the coin toss, but flight that day was not to be. Wilbur made a series of mistakes, and the plane crash-landed. However, the brothers did not give up.

After making some repairs and adjustments, the Wright brothers tried again. This time it was Orville's turn to pilot the plane. On December 17, 1903, at Kitty Hawk, North Carolina, Orville Wright flew the Wright aircraft for 12 seconds and 120 feet (36.5 meters). The brothers flew three more times that day, covering more distance with each flight. Through their teamwork, they made history.

the disease. They then built entire towns to house the workers. Workers stepped up their efforts to build the canal. They used steam shovels to dig into the earth, sometimes removing 200 trainloads a day. They poured cement. They worked machinery. Finally, their hard work paid off. On August 15, 1914, the Panama Canal opened for business.

INVENTION AND INNOVATION

The United States has also benefited from the innovation of people who dreamed big. These people used teamwork to make their dreams a reality. In doing so, they changed the way people in their own time lived. Their inventions paved the way for modern technological advances.

Perhaps the biggest dreamer in U.S. history was Thomas Alva Edison. Edison invented the incandescent lightbulb, the phonograph, and the motion-picture camera, among other things. However, he didn't invent alone. Edison worked with a team of researchers, engineers, laboratory assistants, and other workers. Of his employees, Edison famously said, "If I could do it all alone, I would." Without the people who supported his work, Edison would not have been able to accomplish as much as he did.

Another dreamer was Henry Ford. Ford started his career working as an engineer for Thomas Edison. He left Edison's company to start an automobile company of his own. In 1908, Henry Ford introduced the Model T automobile to the American public. The car was immediately popular, but Ford wanted to do better. He wanted to make it affordable. In 1913, workers at the Ford Motor Company began building Model T Ford automobiles on an assembly line system. Workers stood in place, each adding one part to the automobile as it moved down the line. By building cars in this way, the company could produce more cars for less money. Suddenly, the average person could afford to own an automobile. As a result, Ford Motor Company quickly grew into the world's largest

The teamwork involved in a Ford assembly line made building cars faster and cheaper, which made automobiles more affordable to the average person in the early 1910s. Above, women work outdoors on an early Ford assembly line circa 1913.

automobile manufacturer. Henry Ford used teamwork as an efficient manufacturing system. Because of Ford's innovation, the Ford Motor Company became one of America's greatest successes.

FIGHTING FOR RESPECT

"Freedom is this duty to respect all people, even though they don't love you, they don't respect you, but you respect them and you feel somehow that they can become better than they are."

—Dr. Martin Luther King Jr. (1929–1968),
Baptist minister and civil rights leader

In 1956, Dr. Martin Luther King Jr. spoke the words above in a speech at the Holt Street Baptist Church in Montgomery, Alabama. The year before, Rosa Parks had broken the law when she refused to give up her seat at the front of a bus to a white person. Dr. King and others led the African-American community in boycotting the Montgomery bus system. City officials retaliated and tried to block black citizens from car-pooling. Racial tensions and violence between blacks and whites erupted. In the speech, Dr. King urged his followers to protest peacefully. He pointed out that segregation gives "the persons who are segregated a false sense of inferiority, and it gives those who are sitting up to the front of the bus, on the basis of the fact that they are white, a false sense of superior-ity." Dr. King argued that the goal of the protest was to level the positions, not to reverse them. The only way to do that,

Throughout history people have come together to use teamwork to make positive changes happen in a peaceful way. Dr. Martin Luther King Jr. (*left*) is seen here outlining boycott strategies to advisors and organizers, including civil rights leader Rev. Ralph Abernathy (*left, seated*) and Rosa Parks (*center, seated*) in 1956.

according to King, was for black citizens to show respect to those who disrespected them.

Soon after King's speech, a Supreme Court decision to end segregation on public transportation went into effect. This decision helped fuel other battles in the fight for civil rights. The Montgomery bus boycott is just one example of the struggles people of different groups have faced while trying to gain respect. Throughout history, people have come together using teamwork to protest inequality and discrimination. They have endured violence and hardship and sacrificed their freedom for what they believed was right. Their actions took great courage. They stood up for themselves with self-respect and the belief that all people are entitled to "life, liberty, and the pursuit of happiness" as promised by the founding documents of our government.

AFRICAN AMERICANS AND RESPECT

African Americans have been seeking respect in the United States since its earliest days. White landowners created a thriving economy by exploiting the free labor of enslaved Africans. Some whites became wealthy while many African Americans suffered.

In the 1800s, there was a growing number of people, both black and white, who worked to end slavery in the United States. Abolitionists, who wanted to "abolish" (or end) slavery, joined together to form groups. They based their argument to end slavery on the Bible's call to "Do onto others as you would have them do onto you." This idea is otherwise known as the Golden Rule. Abolitionists created newspapers dedicated to their cause and gave speeches persuading others to join them. Some helped people escape slavery on the Underground Railroad, a network of people who helped slaves escape to the North and Canada.

Following the Civil War, African Americans had freedom but still struggled to find respect. One freedman (as newly freed slaves were called), Houston Hartsfield Holloway, wrote, "For we colored people did not know how to be free and the white people did not know how to have a free colored person about them." The government took steps to help freedmen during the era known as Reconstruction, the period after the Civil War when the U.S. government focused on resolving the aftermath of the war. It built schools to help freed blacks learn to read and write and provided services to provide food, clothing, medical care, and jobs. The government also passed three amendments to the Constitution, granting African Americans legal rights and African-American men the right to vote. During this time, more than 500 African Americans won election to state offices.

All of the progress toward building respect for African Americans began to backslide after Reconstruction ended in 1877. Southern states had resented the Reconstruction laws. The states soon began to take away many of the freedoms that African Americans had enjoyed under Reconstruction. Jim Crow laws—a system that made segregation, or separation, of the races legal—went into effect.

On June 7, 1892, a 30-year-old black shoemaker named Homer Plessy was jailed for sitting in the "white" car of the East Louisiana Railroad. Plessy was one-eighth black and seven-eighths white, but under Louisiana law, he was required to sit in the "colored" (black) car. Plessy went to court and argued that the Separate Car Act violated the Constitution. The judge, John H. Ferguson, did not support Plessy, saying that separating races did not mean that they were not equal. Thus "separate but equal" became the rule of the land.

During this time, racial violence and lynching, or executing people without lawfully convicting them of crimes, rose sharply. Between 1889 and 1930, more than 3,700 men and women were lynched in the United States. The majority of those lynched were Southern blacks.

Segregation of races became commonplace in the United States. Blacks and whites drank from separate water fountains, used separate bathrooms, sat in separate parts of buses, and attended separate schools. Following World War II, there was renewed interest in ending segregation. Beginning in 1950, lawyers from the National Association for the Advancement of Colored People (NAACP) fought to desegregate a school in Charleston, South Carolina. This case and others, collectively called *Brown v. the Board of Education*, went all the way to the United States Supreme Court. In 1954, the Supreme Court unanimously ruled that separate schools provided unequal education. The U.S. Supreme Court admitted that the Court in 1896 had made a mistake in the

Plessy ruling. As mentioned previously, admitting mistakes is a way of showing respect for others. The ruling was a landmark victory for African Americans and it jumpstarted the modern civil rights movement.

Blacks and whites joined together in the civil rights movement to gain equal rights for African-American citizens. They organized sit-ins (when protesters staged a sort of sit-down strike in businesses), marches, and protests, boycotted unfair business, and created a large-scale media campaign to change the hearts and minds of all Americans. Their courageous work achieved great successes, including the passage of the Civil Rights Act of 1964, the Voting Rights Act of 1965, and the Civil Rights Act of 1968. But these successes came at the cost of many lives fighting for the cause, including Dr. Martin Luther King Jr. Today, black Americans have equal protections under the law, but many feel that the struggle for respect continues.

THE WOMEN'S MOVEMENT

Today, women in the United States have more opportunities than at any other time in history. In 2000–2001, women earned 57 percent of all the bachelor's degrees and 59 percent of master's degrees in our country. In that same year, women accounted for 45 percent of all doctorates earned, up from 16 percent 30 years before. Women have successful careers as doctors, lawyers, astronauts, computer scientists, engineers, politicians, and CEOs. This was not the case just 30 years ago. These new opportunities available to women are a sign of increased respect for women in society. However, they did not appear on their own. Throughout history, courageous groups of women have fought to have their voices heard.

In 1776, Abigail Adams wrote a letter to her husband, John, who was working on the Declaration of Independence. She asked that the Continental Congress "remember the ladies." The declaration instead left women out, stating only that "all men are created equal." Early in our nation's history, women enjoyed very few rights. Married women were considered the property of their husbands. Before getting married, women belonged to their fathers. Husbands had the right to imprison or beat their wives as they wished. Women did not have access to higher education or good-paying jobs. They were not allowed to vote. In essence, women's entire lives depended on men supporting them.

On July 13, 1848, a group of five women gathered together in upstate New York: Lucretia Mott, Martha C. Wright, Mary A. McClintock, Jane Hunt, and Elizabeth Cady Stanton. Over tea, they discussed the poor position of women in society. Their conversations were not new—these kinds of discussions had taken place between women for ages. The difference is that these women decided to try to change things.

Within two days, the group had organized a convention "to discuss the social, civil, and religious condition and the rights of women." Stanton drafted a document called "The Declaration of Sentiments" to be discussed at the convention. In it, she used the model of the Declaration of Independence to call for full civil rights for women. Stanton demanded respect for women's voices, including granting women the right to vote.

On July 19–20, 1848, a crowd of about 300 people gathered at Seneca Falls, New York, for the first women's rights convention. Participants debated Stanton's declaration, and eventually, 100 of them agreed to sign it. A media backlash began immediately. Stanton and the other convention organizers were criticized and ridiculed in the press. The names of people who had signed the declaration were released. Some were so embarrassed that they removed their names.

Soon, however, there was a backlash to the backlash. People were disgusted with the negative tone of the press. Instead of discouraging the women's movement, the media actually inspired people to join it. All around the country, people organized their own conventions to speak out for women's rights.

In 1870, African-American men were granted the right to vote under the Fifteenth Amendment. The language of the amendment specifically excluded women from the vote. Not until 1920 would women finally earn the right to elect their own leaders. That right was granted 72 years after the convention at Seneca Falls.

In 1923, activist Alice Paul proposed an Equal Rights Amendment to the Constitution that would ensure that "men and women have equal rights throughout the United States."

The women's suffrage movement called for respect and equality for women. In this image from 1913, a team of women prepares to get the message out on Wall Street, the financial district in New York City, by handing out leaflets demanding that women have the right to vote.

It did not become law. In the 1960s, a second wave of women activists fought for equal education, jobs, pay, and opportunities for women. In the 1970s they picked up Paul's cause and tried to pass the Equal Rights Amendment. The ERA did not pass, but the women's rights movement achieved significant advances for women—advances that are still felt to this day.

LATINOS UNITE

Today, Latinos make up the largest minority group in the United States. Recent political debates about immigration have prompted Latino groups from different cultures to join together and have their voices heard. In 2006, tens of thousands of Latinos gathered in Washington, D.C., to protest the government's proposed plan to arrest illegal immigrants and charge them with a felony. The groups argued that immigrants contribute to society and pay taxes and should be given "a path to citizenship." As a result of the protests, the new law did not pass. However, the topic of illegal immigration remains a hot-button political issue.

Latinos may be on the verge of a new civil rights movement in the United States. However, this is not the first time Latinos have demanded respect. In the 1960s, a group called the Community Service Organization (CSO), led by Cesar Chavez, fought for Latino civil rights. Chavez also wanted to improve the working conditions for some of the poorest people in society—migrant agricultural workers.

In 1962, Chavez left the CSO to found the National Farm Workers Association, now called the United Farm Workers of America. For more than 30 years, Chavez fought to earn migrant farmworkers respect, fair wages, and benefits. He organized boycotts, marches, and peaceful protests. Because of his hard work and dedication to fairness and respect for all people, the plight of farmworkers gained national attention. For the first time in U.S. history, the agricultural industry agreed to labor contracts for farmworkers. Chavez's

Dedicated to fairness, respect, and equality, Cesar Chavez organized groups of migrant farm workers to make their voices heard and bring attention to their plight. Above, Chavez (*center*) poses with grape pickers in support of the United Farm Workers Union in 1968.

work not only improved the lives of farm workers, it inspired generations of Latinos to stand up and demand respect. In the words of Chavez, *"sí se puede"* ("it can be done").

A NATIVE AMERICAN PROTEST

Some historians would point out that since the first Europeans stepped onto North American soil, Native Americans have suffered abuse and disrespect. As white settlers claimed growing amounts of land, they forced Native Americans from their homes and onto remote reservations. On November 9, 1969, a group of Native Americans known as the "Indians of All Tribes" sought to symbolically claim a small patch of land back from the U.S. government. To do it, they took over Alcatraz Island in San Francisco Bay.

Alcatraz once housed a federal prison where many Native Americans had been held. In 1963, the government closed the prison and abandoned the island. The prison's buildings remained intact.

Led by a young Mohawk Indian named Richard Oaks, the Indians of All Tribes sneaked onto the abandoned island in the night. The 100 Indians in the group set up a mini-society right away. Everyone had a job to do—daycare, cleaning, cooking, and security were all assigned to people on the island. A council of members negotiated with the U.S. government. It demanded the government grant the deed to the island, establish a Native American university, and build a cultural center and museum. The government refused to meet the Native Americans' demands.

This occupation of Alcatraz lasted two years. Eventually, the occupiers were forced off the island. The government never met their demands. However, the Alcatraz occupation drew national attention to the issues facing Native Americans. As a result of the occupation, the government changed its discriminatory policies against Native Americans. Alcatraz inspired a political movement for Native American rights that continues today.

Protests by members of the Indians of All Tribes movement, including the group's takeover of Alcatraz, garnered a great deal of attention and influenced the U.S. government to change its policies against Native Americans. Here, members of the movement stand in front of the prison in November 1969. They demanded a visit by the U.S. Secretary of Interior to discuss taking over the land.

A CHEROKEE CHIEF

The Indian occupation of Alcatraz Island had a tremendous effect on a young Cherokee woman named Wilma Mankiller. At the time, Mankiller lived in San Francisco. Her brother and sister went to live on Alcatraz. Although she did not live there with them, Mankiller was proud of her siblings and the occupation. In her 1994 autobiography, *Mankiller: A Chief and Her People*, Mankiller writes, "Every day that passed [on Alcatraz] seemed to give me more self-respect and sense of pride."

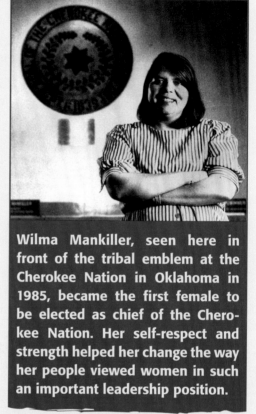

Wilma Mankiller, seen here in front of the tribal emblem at the Cherokee Nation in Oklahoma in 1985, became the first female to be elected as chief of the Cherokee Nation. Her self-respect and strength helped her change the way her people viewed women in such an important leadership position.

This event sparked Mankiller's interest in politics. In 1983, she won election as deputy chief of the Cherokee Nation of Oklahoma. Two years later, Mankiller became the first female chief of the Cherokee Nation. "Prior to my election, young Cherokee girls would never have thought that they might grow up to be chief," wrote Mankiller.

Mankiller faced discrimination from people who did not think a woman should be chief, but she always believed in herself. Mankiller's self-respect and determination helped change the way Cherokees viewed leadership. She writes in her book *Mankiller*, "Today if anyone asks members of our tribe if it really matters if the chief is male or female, the majority will reply that gender has no bearing on leadership." Although Mankiller retired from the role of chief in 1995, she remains one of the Cherokee Nation's most respected leaders.

RESPECT AROUND THE WORLD

People all around the world have fought and continue to fight for respect. Their struggles show that human beings are strong, courageous, and deserving of respect everywhere in the world. They remind us that respect is such an important virtue that people are willing to give their lives for it.

Perhaps no other man in history did more for the cause of respect for all than Mohandas (Mahatma) Gandhi. Martin Luther King Jr. and Cesar Chavez both followed Gandhi's teachings of "nonviolent resistance." To say that Gandhi "fought" for respect is not quite right. Instead, Gandhi and his followers peacefully resisted the government. Gandhi first

Mohandas (Mahatma) Gandhi encouraged nonviolent protests in order to bring about positive change, such as the independence of India from England. Here, Gandhi (*under the arrow*) breaks the salt laws—which gave the British government a monopoly over salt production—in 1930 by peacefully working with volunteers to pick up natural salt that had been deposited in a pit.

used his methods in South Africa, where he got the government to treat Indian immigrants more fairly. Then the tiny Indian man took on the mighty British government, which controlled India. Eventually, India gained independence, in part because of Gandhi's leadership. On January 30, 1948, Gandhi was assassinated, but his influence and spirit live on to this day.

In the late 1970s and 1980s, Lech Walesa fought to gain respect for Polish workers. At the time, Poland was under the control of the Soviet Union's (modern-day Russia's) communist government. Under Soviet rule, people worked long hours in poor conditions. Walesa organized a union of workers known as Solidarity to stand up to the Soviet Union. The word *solidarity* means community or coming together. Like Gandhi before him, Walesa encouraged nonviolent

ANNE FRANK AND THE FOUR HELPERS

In 1942, when Anne Frank was 13 years old, her family moved into a hidden attic above her father's business. The Franks were German Jews living in the Netherlands. At that time, Adolf Hitler and the Nazis were sending Jewish people to labor camps. The Nazis eventually killed 6 million Jews during World War II at these concentration camps. The Frank family chose to hide rather than be sent away to the camps.

Four courageous people helped the Franks and another family hide: Miep Gies, Victor Kugler, Bep Voskuijl, and Johanness Kleimann. By helping Jewish people, the helpers broke Nazi law. They risked prison, deportation, or even death if caught. Gies later said, "In those dark days during the war, we didn't stand on the sidelines. We offered a helping hand. We committed our very lives. We couldn't have done any more than that."

Each of the helpers had a job to do. Johanness and Victor ran Mr. Frank's business downstairs. They also brought books and magazines protest. The Soviets jailed Walesa, but he did not give up. Eventually, the Soviet government negotiated better conditions for the workers. In 1983, Walesa was awarded the Nobel Peace Prize. In 1990, he won election as Poland's president. He served as president until 1995. Today, Poland is completely free from the Soviet government's control.

In 1989, a different group of people protested communism, this time in China. Between April 15 and June 4, different groups of people around China held peaceful protests against the communist government. The government responded by arresting protesters and sending in the Chinese military to end the protests.

In Tiananmen Square in Beijing, the clash between citizens and government reached a boiling point. Late in the day on June 3, military tanks rolled into Tiananmen Square and

for the hiders. Bep brought bread and milk. Miep brought meat and vegetables along with news of the outside world. The helpers had to be careful. If anyone suspected they were helping Jewish families, they would certainly be caught.

The hiders had to be silent during the day so the workers in the factory downstairs would not hear them. They could not even go to the bathroom. Anne found comfort in writing. She recorded all of her thoughts in her diary.

Anne and her family lived in the attic for two years. Then on August 4, 1944, Nazi soldiers stormed into the attic. Someone had reported the hiders. The Nazis sent every person in the attic to concentration camps. Only Anne's father, Otto Frank, survived.

Miep Gies saved Anne's beloved diary. In it, Anne shows her faith in humanity despite the world around her. "I still believe, in spite of everything, that people are truly good at heart," she wrote. The diary was later published as a book, *Anne Frank: The Diary of a Young Girl.*

In 1980, Lech Walesa cofounded the first trade union for workers in Soviet Bloc countries, which then included the Soviet Union (Russia) and countries it controlled or counted among its allies (including Walesa's home country of Poland). Above, Walesa speaks to striking workers at Lenin Shipyard in Gdansk, Poland, in 1988.

fired on the crowd. Hundreds of protesters, many of them college students, were killed. The situation in China today has not improved, but students still dare to protest, and the government knows that they have to listen to the protesters.

ATHLETES AND TEAMWORK

7

"The strength of the team is each individual member . . . the strength of each member is the team."

—*Phil Jackson (1945–), NBA basketball coach*

Every successful athlete uses teamwork to help achieve a personal best. Sometimes the teamwork is obvious. For example, the players on a basketball team may work together to set up the perfect three-point shot. The fans watching the game can clearly see the teamwork involved. Other times, the teamwork is behind the scenes. For example, a tennis player may compete on the court alone. However, the coach, trainer, nutritionist, doctor, family, and any number of other people work together to prepare the player to perform his or her best.

No athlete succeeds alone. That is why athletics provide a unique opportunity to study teamwork. Whereas in business a person may go against the team and still be able to achieve goals, in sports every member of the team must work together or else the team fails. Teammates who do not get along personally must learn to set aside their differences for the good of the sport. Many people can recall a time when the players on their favorite sports team came together to score an important point or pull off an unlikely victory. In sports, good teamwork excites spectators. We cheer at the victories and gasp at the near misses. We feel our hearts pounding with the thrill of each play. Next time you watch a sports event, study how the players use teamwork. Think about how you can apply the lessons of your favorite sports teams to your own life.

TEAMWORK IN BASEBALL

Baseball is a uniquely American sport. In fact, baseball is often referred to as America's pastime. Throughout our history, excited fans have crowded into ballparks to cheer on their favorite baseball teams. And sometimes, those teams achieved remarkable feats and became legendary.

That was certainly the case during the 2004 World Series when the Boston Red Sox played the St. Louis Cardinals in St.

JACKIE ROBINSON AND THE BROOKLYN DODGERS

It was more than 60 years ago that Jackie Robinson stepped onto Ebbets Field to play for the Brooklyn Dodgers. That day in 1947 Jackie Robinson put on his number-42 uniform and made history. For the first time since the 1800s, an African American played baseball in the major leagues.

Robinson faced enormous pressure in his first year. If he failed, he would doom the chances of future black athletes being allowed to play. While some fans were excited to see Jackie play, others sent him hate mail and death threats. Rival teams did not want to share the field with him. At first, even Robinson's own teammates hoped he would fail. Robinson stood up for himself. He said to his teammates, "I'm not concerned with your liking or disliking me. All I ask is that you respect me as a human being. Regardless of how you feel about me, I hope we can work together on the field. Thank you."

Louis. That year, the Sox swept all four games of the series, earning their first World Series victory since 1918.

Red Sox fans everywhere celebrated as their team defeated "the curse of the Bambino." Generations of fans had passed on the story of the fateful day that the Sox traded Babe Ruth (*bambino* means "baby boy" or "babe" in Italian) to the rival team, the New York Yankees. Ever since then, the Sox had been unable to bring home a championship, while the Yankees won series after series.

Leading up to the series, the Sox played four straight games against the rival Yankees in the American League Championships. The players kept their focus on getting to the series and on bringing home victory for the fans. Once they got there, the Sox easily won the title. For the first time in most of their fans' lifetimes, the Boston Red Sox were

After playing ball with Robinson, his teammates did come to like and respect him.

In his first year, Robinson played impressively. In 1947, *The Sporting News*, a paper that had been against blacks in the major leagues, awarded Robinson its first Rookie of the Year award. Robinson went on to become one of baseball's greatest athletes. He helped the Dodgers win six pennants and one World Series. Jackie Robinson was entered into the Baseball Hall of Fame in 1962.

The Brooklyn Dodgers are now the Los Angeles Dodgers, but the spirit of Jackie Robinson lives on. The Jackie Robinson Foundation, established in Robinson's honor, provides scholarships to help minorities attend college. Robinson's story of breaking baseball's color barrier has inspired millions of people to reach for their dreams, however impossible they may seem.

The success of a sports team depends on teamwork and the effort of each player on that team. In 2004, the Boston Red Sox were able to win their first World Series victory since 1918. Here, they celebrate after their 3-0 win in game four of the series against the St. Louis Cardinals.

champions. But, just to prove the curse was officially broken, the Sox won the World Series again in 2007.

AMAZING MOMENTS IN TEAMWORK

There are some moments in history where teamwork stands out above all else; times when teammates work in harmony and beat impossible odds. These emotional moments are triumphs of the human spirit. They show us that, with determination and commitment, people working together can achieve their wildest dreams.

Reaching New Heights

One such moment happened on May 29, 1953. On that day, British mountain climber Sir Edmund Hillary and his partner Tenzig Norgay, a Nepali Sherpa (Sherpas are Tibetan people who live on the slopes of the Himalayas and are known for providing support to foreign adventurers), became the first people to reach the top of Mt. Everest, the highest point on Earth.

The two partners had begun the expedition with a group of climbers. After another two-man team failed to reach the summit, Sir Edmund and Tenzig set out to try it for themselves. To get to the top, the two climbers tied themselves together

In 1953, Edmund P. Hillary and Tenzing Norgay worked together to do what no person had ever done before: climb to the top of Mt. Everest. Above, they stand in front of the British Embassy in Nepal a month after their climb, outfitted as they were during their historic journey.

and used ice picks to carve out toeholds in the steep mountain rock. After almost falling a few times, the climbers finally reached the summit. "The whole world around us lay spread out like a giant relief map," Sir Edmund said. "I am a lucky man. I have had a dream and it has come true, and that is not a thing that happens often to men." Since that historic day, some 3,000 people have stood atop Everest, and more than 200 have died trying to make the climb. Sir Edmund Hillary and Tenzig Norgay are remembered for their bravery and teamwork.

The Magnificent Seven

At the 1996 Summer Olympics in Atlanta, Georgia, seven American gymnasts achieved their own amazing teamwork

The United States women's gymnastics team overcame huge obstacles to be awarded gold medals in the 1996 Summer Olympic Games in Atlanta, Georgia.

AN UNDERDOG TEAM, A "GIANT" VICTORY

It was the catch seen 'round the world. With 35 seconds left in the fourth quarter of Super Bowl XLII, New York Giants wide receiver David Tyree did the impossible. He leaped into the air and caught a pass from quarterback Eli Manning, pressing the ball to his helmet as New England Patriots safety Rodney Harrison leapt for an interception. Moments before, Manning had escaped getting sacked in order to make the throw to Tyree and secure a 17-14 victory over the Patriots.

No one expected it to end this way. The Patriots were the clear favorites. They were 18-0 and were expected to make it a perfect 19-0 season. Most experts favored Patriots quarterback Tom Brady over Manning. The odds against them, the Giants did not give up. "We believed the whole time," said Manning. And so,

Though the New England Patriots were the clear favorites, the New York Giants stepped up their game to win Superbowl XLII in 2008. Here, David Tyree jumps in front of Patriot Rodney Harrison to catch a pass from teammate Eli Manning, securing victory for the Giants over the Patriots in an exciting display of good teamwork.

the team worked together, sacking Brady five times and slowing the Patriots' offense for much of the game. "We did it to prove to ourselves we could do it," Giants defensive end Michael Strahan, who retired

(continues)

(continued)

after the win, said. "We were stopping the best offense in football. Of course, they were surprised. We shocked the world. We shocked ourselves."

Manning was awarded MVP (most valuable player) for his contribution to the game. However, it was the combined efforts of the entire team that allowed the underdogs from New York to achieve a giant victory.

moment. They were dubbed the Magnificent Seven: Shannon Miller, Dominique Dawes, Kerri Strug, Dominique Moceanu, Jaycie Phelps, Amy Chow, and Amanda Borden.

In the vaulting event, Moceanu fell twice. Then Strug stepped up to the vault. On her first vault, Strug fell too, severely injuring her ankle. Rather than give up her team's chances at gold, Strug chose to vault again and landed a near-perfect jump. Then she collapsed to the floor in pain. In part because of Strug's vault, the American women's gymnastics team won its first-ever Olympic gold medal. Team captain Amanda Borden said, "Kerri made an unbelievable move. She came through when it counted." In 2008, the team was nominated to join the U.S. Olympic Hall of Fame.

CHAMPIONS OF TEAMWORK

Real teamwork, of course, is more than brief moments of glory. It is about working hard and sticking together through thick and thin. Real teamwork is about celebrating successes and learning from mistakes. It cannot be measured in one game or even in one season, but over the course of a career.

Michael Jordan

Michael Jordan's work with the Chicago Bulls is a perfect example of a career of admirable teamwork. Jordan played for

Michael Jordan is often named among the best professional basketball players in the history of the sport, but he couldn't have done as well with out the support of his teammates. Above, Jordan's teammate in the Chicago Bulls, Dennis Rodman (*center*), clears the way for Jordan by blocking Jeff Hornacek of the Utah Jazz during a 1998 NBA Finals Game.

more than 10 years with the Bulls, helping them win 6 NBA (National Basketball Association) Championships and himself winning 5 NBA MVP awards. Jordan credits his success to his team. In his 1999 book, *Michael Jordan Speaks: Lessons from the World's Greatest Champion*, Jordan writes, "Talent wins games, but teamwork and intelligence wins championships."

Jordan has been called the greatest basketball player of all time, but he has always remained humble about his talent. In his 1998 autobiography, *For the Love of the Game: My Story*, he writes, "There is no such thing as a perfect basketball player, and I don't believe there is only one greatest player either. Everyone plays in different eras. I built my talents on the shoulders of someone else's talent. I believe greatness is an evolutionary process that changes and evolves era to era. Without Julius Erving, David Thompson, Walter Davis, and Elgin Baylor there would never have been a Michael Jordan. I evolved from them." For Jordan, even past players belong to his team.

Jordan continues to work hard today to be a good role model for young people and continues to support his community with special concern for minority and underprivileged children. Among other charitable pursuits, he started the James R. Jordan Boys & Girls Club and Family Life Center in Chicago in honor of his father.

Venus and Serena Williams

Although they have often competed against one another, Venus and Serena Williams consider themselves lifelong teammates. The sisters have been playing tennis since they were just six years old. Both are impressive players. Through October 2008, Venus won 38 career singles titles, while Serena (one year younger) won 32. Playing together, the sisters have won Olympic gold medals in 2000 and 2008. Venus and Serena push one another to be their best. In 1999, Serena said, "Whatever my potential is, I want to reach it—now. And if I do, I see Venus as my biggest competition." The Williams

Though they have competed against one another, tennis star sisters Venus (*right*) and Serena Williams often serve as teammates. Above, they celebrate after winning the doubles final at Wimbledon in 2008.

sisters both showcase their individual talent and work as a team to succeed together.

Tiger Woods

The partnership between Tiger Woods and his dad, Earl Woods, was often discussed when the elder Woods was alive because he attended nearly all of his son's key tournaments. In 2008, Tiger payed tribute to the man who had been his teammate behind the scenes. Earl died of cancer in May 2006. At the Tiger Woods Learning Center, near where father and son used to practice, Tiger unveiled a bronze statue of himself and his dad. Woods said the statue honors his father's unwavering support. "He was always there. That's basically what it symbolizes. He always had my back. If I failed, I could always come home to love," he said.

With the coaching and support of his dad, Tiger Woods has become one of the finest golf players in history. Now a father himself, Woods said he will continue his father's traditions with his own child.

MODERN MODELS 8 OF TEAMWORK AND RESPECT

> "Never doubt that a small group of thoughtful, committed citizens can change the world. Indeed, it's the only thing that ever has."
> —*Margaret Mead (1901–1979), American anthropologist*

There are plenty of examples of people fighting and disrespecting one another. From parents and kids who don't listen to each other to bullies and their victims in school, disrespect is easy to recognize. We also see it on reality TV shows where people get rejected week after week, as millions of viewers tune in to see if their favorites win and their "favorites" to lose really do lose. This kind of entertainment may be fun to watch, but it is also mean-spirited and hurtful, and it is not much different from how a bully acts at school. Some people may argue that those in the public eye deserve whatever kind of attention they get, but the truth is that people do not stop having feelings just because they are famous, even if just for a few minutes on television.

Fortunately, if you look closely at the world around, you can find tremendous examples of teamwork and respect, too. Today, people who celebrate these virtues can be found across the country and the world. Young people develop teamwork and respect on Boy Scout or Girl Scout camping trips and community youth groups. Businesses put together teams of employees to work on projects. Volunteer organizations bring people together to promote the greater good. Even entire countries come together to solve the world's problems. There is always an opportunity to be part of a great team for anyone who cares to join one.

MAKING A DIFFERENCE

It is no secret that teamwork helps groups of people get things done. Yet, it may surprise you to know that committed people around the globe are using teamwork to change the world. From organizing natural disaster relief efforts to solving global problems, people are joining together to make a difference.

Large sections of the U.S. Gulf Coast were destroyed after Hurricane Katrina struck parts of Mississippi, Louisiana, and Florida—among other states—in August 2005. Since then, more than 1.1 million Americans have volunteered their time and energy to help rebuild the Gulf Coast. They have cleared debris, hammered nails, and installed drywall.

Still, some things are more difficult to repair because the damage is harder to see. Louisiana has a rich musical history and culture. It is the unofficial home of jazz music. Many of New Orleans's great musicians lost their homes in the hurricane. That is why respected jazz musicians Harry Connick Jr. and Branford Marsalis teamed up with Habitat for Humanity to build the Musician's Village in New Orleans. Volunteers from around the country have come together to help build the village. When complete, Musician's Village will contain 72 single-family homes for musicians and their families. In addition, the village will have a cultural center for musicians to play and students to learn about New Orleans's rich history. The village seeks to rebuild not only the buildings but also the spirit of New Orleans.

People volunteer time and energy for great causes every day. The two volunteers pictured above were volunteering on behalf of Habitat for Humanity in 2007 to rebuild houses in New Orleans that were destroyed by Hurricane Katrina.

In 2004, a group of nonprofit, advocacy, and humanitarian organizations joined together with individual citizens to form the ONE campaign. The goal of the campaign is to end extreme poverty and AIDS around the globe. The ONE campaign uses the collective voice of its members to persuade the U.S. government to provide more assistance to countries in need. In 2004, the Bill and Melinda Gates Foundation pledged $3 million to the campaign. By 2008, more than 2.8 million people from all 50 states and 100 organizations had joined, and those numbers continue to grow. New members can sign up at *www.one.org* to pledge to help "make poverty history."

Like the ONE campaign, the Global Health Council is a network of organizations that joined together for the greater good. It is the largest membership organization dedicated to solving global health problems in the world. The Global Health Council works to improve the health of the world's citizens, especially in areas of extreme poverty. For example, more than 10 million children die each year before the age of 5, mostly from preventable causes, such as unclean drinking water, malnutrition, and malaria. That is about 300,000 children dying every single day. The Global Health Council

A MARINE ON A MISSION

When Marine Captain Brian Steidle volunteered to travel to the African country of Sudan as a military observer in 2004, he thought he was accepting a job. Instead Steidle discovered his life's mission: to stop the killing in Darfur. The Sudanese government has been in conflict with the people of its Darfur region since 2003. The government, along with a group of rebel fighters called the Janjaweed, burn Darfur villages, shoot villagers, and sexually assault women in the region. The United Nations estimates that 200,000 people in Darfur have died as a result of the violence and illness related to the conflict. The United States has labeled the killing genocide, or the deliberate killing of a group of people.

Steidle was one of very few Americans inside Darfur in the first years of the conflict. Armed with only his camera, Steidle photographed the violence in the region. After six months, Steidle returned home. He needed to show the world what he had seen. Upon returning, Steidle spoke out to the U.S. government, to news organizations, and to citizens around the country. He urged leaders to take more action against Sudan. A 2007 documentary called *The Devil Came on Horseback* shares Steidle's experiences with a world audience. Despite efforts of people around the world, the violence in Darfur continues as of 2008.

is working with other organizations to lower child deaths by two-thirds by the year 2015. The council also is working to improve other world health problems such as HIV/AIDS, women's health, infectious diseases, and emerging threats. By working together, members of the Global Health Council are enacting real change in the lives of people around the world.

BUSINESS AND TECHNOLOGY

There are many great examples of teamwork and respect in the business world, too. Some of today's best-known companies were built on the commitment to respect employees as well as the communities that they serve. Other companies have used teamwork to develop innovative products that are changing the way we live our lives.

One company tops them all for team innovation and respect for employees. For two years running, Google has been named #1 Best Company to Work for by *Fortune* magazine. Google makes sure that every employee knows that he or she is an important part of the team. No role has more or less value than any other, and that makes everyone feel respected. At the company's headquarters in Mountain View, California, Google employees enjoy workout facilities, massage therapists, and even a game room with video games and foosball. Throughout the day, a cart comes by with healthy snacks for employees. Employees are encouraged to take breaks on couches set up in the offices. They can even bring their dogs to work.

Google believes that happy employees are the key to the company's success. At lunchtime, it is not unusual for groups to gather to brainstorm their latest ideas. This policy has helped Google to grow into one of the world's most well-known companies. The company's search engine is so popular that people now say they have "googled" something when they mean they searched the Web. Google's management team knows that respect and teamwork go hand-in-hand.

THE GOOGLE GUYS

Larry Page and Sergey Brin are just average American guys that happen to be self-made billionaires. When Page and Brin met as college students at Stanford University, they never dreamed they would create the world's most used Internet search engine. They didn't even like each other that much at first.

Things changed when Page and Brin teamed up to build a search engine for their college dormitory. The partners soon found that their engine might be useful outside of school. They borrowed money from family, friends, and investors to start their company. In 1998, Page and Brin launched Google from a friend's garage. From there, the company has grown into a worldwide empire. The founders have a simple motto that they follow as the company expands, "Don't be evil." The Google guys use respect as a guiding principle, and it shows.

If Google changed the way we use the Web, Apple Inc. changed the way we use computers. From MP3 players to cell phones to laptops, the team at Apple Inc. is always on the cutting edge of new technology. Steve Jobs, the CEO and cofounder of Apple, challenges his team of employees to dream big and pushes them hard to achieve results. In 2000, Apple introduced the iPod, which became the world's most popular MP3 player. In 2007, the Apple team released the first iPhone, which combines a cell phone, the Web, a camera, and an MP3 player into one handy little device. In 2008, Apple introduced the world's thinnest laptop, MacBook Air. Because of its innovation, *Fortune* magazine named Apple Inc. #1 Most Admired Company. Nobody knows what Apple will dream up next, but one thing is for sure: Steve Jobs and his team are hard at work developing their next big idea.

People all over the country flock to Starbucks for coffee, but they may not know that Starbucks also has a reputation of respecting its employees. The company was recognized as one of *Fortune* magazine's 100 Best Companies to Work For and as *Business Ethic*'s 100 Best Corporate Citizens.

When Howard Schultz bought Starbucks in 1987, he grew the company based on the principles of respecting employees and giving back to communities where Starbucks stores exist. Toward that, Starbucks offers health benefits to both full-time and part-time employees. The company also provides employees with free coffee and tea products. Through its *Make Your Mark* program, Starbucks encourages its employees to volunteer in their communities. In 2006, Starbucks employees donated more than 383,000 volunteer hours to community projects. In addition, the company donated more than $36.1 million in cash and products to the communities it serves.

INTERNATIONAL TEAMWORK

It is commonly believed that the world is getting smaller—in the sense that it is getting more connected. Countries have become interdependent. Today we have telephones, airplanes, satellites, and the Internet to keep us in contact with people outside our part of the world. We can find out about everything that is happening in the world the instant that it happens. We can trade products and labor back and forth across the globe. We can share our resources to help improve the lives of all humans. We can bring together the world's greatest minds to achieve new scientific breakthroughs. We can share our knowledge with the world. That is the spirit of countries working together through international teamwork.

On October 24, 1945, 51 countries joined together to establish the United Nations. World War II had just ended. There was a strong desire to prevent similar wars in the future. The goal of the organization was to "preserve peace through international cooperation and collective security." Today, 192 countries belong to the United Nations—that is nearly every country on Earth. When representatives from these countries meet at the U.N. Headquarters in New York City, they make important decisions affecting the world. In addition to peacekeeping, the United Nations provides humanitarian assistance to countries in need, establishes trade laws, and prosecutes war criminals. Some people argue that it does not do enough. For example, it has been unable to end the violence in Darfur, Sudan. However, at present the United Nations is the best way to encourage cooperation among nations.

One example of international teamwork did not happen on Earth, but in space. The International Space Station is a complex, scientific laboratory that is being built in outer

The International Space Station proves that incredible things can happen when people from around the world work together. In this image from 2005, crews of the space shuttle *Discovery* and the International Space Station wave. *Discovery* shuttle commander Eileen Collins waves in the upper right. Clockwise from her position are astronaut Charles J. Camarda, Japanese Aerospace Agency astronaut Soichi Noguchi, astronaut Wendy Lawrence, cosmonaut Sergei Krikalev, astronaut James M. Kelly, astronaut Andrew S.W. Thomas, and astronaut John L. Phillips.

space from the inside out. Orbiting 240 miles (386 km) above Earth, the International Space Station is a marvel of engineering that shows what the greatest scientists in the world can accomplish when they join together. When complete, the station will include contributions from 16 nations: the United States, Canada, Japan, Russia, Brazil, Belgium, Denmark, France, Germany, Italy, the Netherlands, Norway, Spain, Sweden, Switzerland, and the United Kingdom.

In 1998, the first part of the station was launched into space. Since 2000, human space crews have been building the rest of the station and conducting scientific experiments there. NASA describes living and working in the space station as "building a one room house, moving in a family of three, and asking them to finish building the house while working a full-time job from home." Crews to the station stay for 6 months and are on call for work 24 hours a day, 7 days a week. When they are not constructing the space station, astronauts are conducting experiments in space. These experiments will help astronauts learn about space and its effects on the human body, among other things. This will help with future space missions farther away from home.

9 BUILD YOUR CHARACTER

"Be the change you wish to see in the world."
—Mohandas Gandhi (1869–1948),
Indian political and spiritual leader

You develop your character through the choices you make. When you choose to behave morally, you develop good character. When you choose to behave immorally, you develop poor character. It is as simple as that.

There is an old expression about character: "Character is what you do when nobody's looking." In other words, having good character is about behaving morally because you believe it is the right thing to do, not because you are trying to prove yourself to someone else. Your character is about you and the choices you make for yourself. It is about the kind of person you want to be. If your parents go out of town and leave you alone, your character will decide whether to follow their rules or whether to disobey them and throw a party. If your friends pressure you to have the party, it is your character that will either give you the courage to stand up to them or allow you to cave to their peer pressure. In the party example, having good character is not about the fear of getting caught—it is about respecting your parents' rules and feeling good about the choices you make.

Having good character sometimes means sacrificing short-term pleasures for long-term fulfillment. Having a party might be fun, but it might also make you feel guilty for lying to your parents. It might make you feel distant from them because you are keeping a secret that would damage their trust in you. In the end, the party could just make you feel bad. On the other hand, you might at first feel badly about not having the party. You might feel like you have let down your friends. Those feelings might change, however, when you consider that you have done a trustworthy action. According to author Thomas Lickona, people with good character develop satisfaction from behaving morally. In other words, not having the party will make you feel good about who you are as a person.

BECOME A TEAM PLAYER

One way to develop your character is to become a team player. Being a "team player" means putting the team first. A team player thinks about his or her responsibilities to the team. A team player is reliable and realizes that teammates depend on him or her just as he or she depends on them. Team players understand that all team members have to do their parts in order for the team to be a winning one. When one member of a team is not a team player, the entire team suffers. That is why employers and employees consider team players to be of such crucial importance.

In fact, whether or not a person is a team player may determine his or her future success in the workforce. In 2003, the University of Connecticut and the Level Playing Field Institute surveyed employers and employees across the country for the HOW-FAIR Study. The study found that both employers and employees ranked "being a team player" as the most important quality for advancing in a company. Being a team player was considered more important than doing a good job, being intelligent, being creative, and even making money for the organization. The study indicates that people who work well on teams have the best chances of getting ahead in life. That is certainly motivation to brush up on your teamwork skills and build your character.

DEMONSTRATE RESPECT

A sure sign of strong character is respect. While it is important to show respect for everyone, there are different ways to show respect for people depending on their relationship to you. A person probably wouldn't tip his or her parents for serving dinner at home but would tip a waiter at a restaurant,

RESPECT FOR OUR PLANET

Respect is a virtue that applies to more than just people. It is also important to respect the world around us. That means taking care of our property, our pets, and our planet.

In 2005, Robert F. Kennedy Jr., Laurie David, and Senator John McCain started the *Stop Global Warming Virtual March* out of respect for our planet. The goal of the march is to join citizens from all over the world to stop global climate change. Science tells us that the Earth is getting warmer because of an increased amount of carbon dioxide in the air. The carbon dioxide acts like a shield, trapping the sun's warmth on the planet. Warmer temperatures may seem nice, but they actually can cause big problems, such as flooding, natural disasters, and habitat destruction for animals.

There are steps that individuals can take to reduce their carbon output. These include using less electricity, using recycled paper, using cloth bags instead of plastic, drinking from reusable water bottles, and more. The *Stop Global Warming Virtual March* is about building a community of committed citizens who pledge to reduce their carbon emissions and help stop global warming. It is about showing respect for the Earth. So far, more than a million people from all 50 states have joined the march. To find out more, visit *www.stopglobalwarming.org*.

for example. Consider the different ways you might show respect for:

* Your parents, stepparents, and guardians
* Other relatives (siblings, grandparents, aunts, and uncles)
* Teachers, coaches, and bosses
* Service workers (waiters, store clerks)
* Neighbors and other adults
* Senior citizens and people in need
* Peers
* Yourself

A good rule to follow is always to consider the feelings and needs of the other person, even if you do not know him or her. For example, welcome new students to class because they might not know anyone yet. Take the initiative at work to tackle that project that needs to be done before your boss asks you to do it. Thank the salesperson for helping you, even though it is his or her job. Volunteer to help your neighbor mow the lawn. Pay attention to the person in front of you, not the cell phone in your hand. Take care of your body, your brain, and your well-being. Surround yourself with supportive friends who love you for you. Demonstrating respect is all about the little things you can do that make a difference in someone's day and even your own.

A PERSON OF CHARACTER

Nikole Evans is a typical college student. She attends class at Western Washington University, hangs out with friends, and loves to travel. Yet, in her spare time, Evans is changing the world. Maybe that doesn't sound typical, but Evans is looking to change that, too.

In kindergarten, Evans became a Daisy Chain Girl Scout and from there began a life devoted to volunteer work. She has done small community projects, such as reading to

LEARN MORE ABOUT GOOD CHARACTER

C heck out these organizations and Web sites that promote team-work and respect.

Giraffe Heroes Project

Since 1984, the Giraffe Heroes Project has honored "human giraffes," or "people who stick their neck out for the common good." This nonprofit organization shares the stories of everyday people who stand up for what is right and help make the world a better place.
www.giraffe.org

Youth Service America

The mission of Youth Service America is to improve the quality and quantity of volunteer and service opportunities for young people, ages 5–25. This resource center partners with thousands of organizations that engage young people.
www.ysa.org

Outward Bound

On Outward Bound courses, students develop self-reliance, responsibility, teamwork, confidence, and compassion by working together on a physi-cally challenging wilderness adventure.
www.outwardboundwilderness.org

Girl Scouts of America

Founded in 1912 by Juliette Gordon Low, the Girl Scouts of America is one of the world's most respected organizations. The Girl Scouts is devoted to developing the character of young women.
www.girlscouts.org

Boy Scouts of America

The Boy Scouts of America is an organization dedicated to help young men "make ethical and moral choices over their lifetimes." Through commu-nity programs, the Boy Scouts helps young men develop their character.
www.scouting.org

children and visiting with the elderly, and big projects, such as providing AIDS/HIV awareness training and starting the antiviolence group Students Against Violence Everywhere.

One of Evans's most memorable projects was working with a team of 11 young people as an AmeriCorps volunteer. AmeriCorps is a national volunteer organization. Evans and her team tutored young people, built houses, and did other service work. The team received an award for completing the most projects of any AmeriCorps team. "We learned by working together, we could do more, and help more people," Evans said of her team.

Evans knows that she can't change the world on her own. That is why, when she was just 13 years old, Evans started the Web site *www.y2kyouth.com*. The Web site lists service opportunities for young people and provides advice to help them begin service projects. She wants to help others learn "how fulfilling and personally rewarding it is when you help someone succeed."

For her work, Evans has won numerous honors and awards. In 1999, the United Nations awarded Evans the Global Youth, Peace, & Tolerance Award. In 2004, the United Nations honored her again, highlighting her in their Building a Culture of Peace Display. Evans has also been honored as a National Youth Peacemaker and a Giraffe Hero, among other honors. She has met four Nobel Peace Laureates—Betty Williams, Nelson Mandela, Mikhail Gorbachev, and Elie Weisel. When asked for her message to other young people looking to make a difference, Evans said, "Make someone happy, make someone smile, help someone. If I can do it, so can you!"

GLOSSARY

assert   To declare positively

confidence   The feeling of being certain

conscience   The sense of morality of one's own conduct

consideration   Thoughtful regard for another person

empathy   Understanding the feelings of another person

enriches   Enhances

groupthink   A pattern of thought when all people conform to the group's ideas

integrity   Firm adherence to moral values

interdependent   Mutually dependent

self-esteem   A confidence and satisfaction in oneself

self-worth   The sense of one's own value or worth

solidarity   Unity as a group

team   A number of persons associated together in work or activity

teammate   A fellow member of a team

teamwork   The cooperative effort by the members of a group or team to achieve a common goal

virtue   A particular moral excellence

virtuous   Morally excellent

BIBLIOGRAPHY

"About Us." New Orleans Habitat Musicians' Village. 2008. Available online. URL: http://www.nolamusiciansvillage. com/about/. Accessed March 15, 2008.

"About Us." Starbucks Coffee Company. Available online. URL: http://www.starbucks.com/aboutus/. Accessed March 15, 2008.

"Acquiring virtue is better than acquiring gold." *Columbia World of Quotations*. 1996. Available online. URL: http://www. bartleby.com/66/46/2246.html. Accessed March 15, 2008.

"The African-American Odyssey: A Quest for Full Citizenship." *American Memory*. Library of Congress. Available online. URL: http://memory.loc.gov/ammem/aaohtml/exhibit/ aointro.html. Accessed March 15, 2008.

"America's Most Admired Companies 2008." *Fortune*, March 3, 2008. Available online. URL: http://money.cnn.com/ magazines/fortune/mostadmired/2008/index.html>. Accessed March 15, 2008.

Anderson, Irving. "The Corps." Lewis and Clark. PBS. Available online. URL: http://www.pbs.org/lewisandclark/inside/idx_ corp.html. Accessed February 23, 2008.

Angelou, Maya. Interview with Linda Wolf. *Daughters of the Moon, Sisters of the Sun*, by Karen Wind Hughes and Linda Wolf. Gabriola Island, B.C.: New Society, 1997. 91.

"Aretha Franklin Biography." *Rolling Stone,* 2001. Available online. URL: http://www.rollingstone.com/artists/ arethafranklin/biography. Accessed March 15, 2008.

"Aristotle's Ethics." *Stanford Encyclopedia of Philosophy*. July 17, 2007. Stanford University. Available online. URL: http:// plato.stanford.edu/entries/aristotle-ethics/. Accessed March 15, 2008.

Banks, James A., et al. *Making a New Nation*. New York: Macmillan/McGraw, 2007.

"The Banks That Robbed the World." *BBC News,* June 9, 2004. Available online. URL: http://news.bbc.co.uk. Accessed February 20, 2008.

"Baseball and Jackie Robinson." *American Memory Collection.* Library of Congress. Available online. URL: http://memory. loc.gov/ammem/collections/robinson/. Accessed March 15, 2008.

Battista, Judy. "Giants Stun Patriots in Super Bowl XLII." *The New York Times,* February 4, 2008. Available online. URL: http://www.nytimes.com. Accessed March 15, 2008.

Bill and Melinda Gates Foundation. 2008. Available online. URL: http://www.gatesfoundation.org. Accessed March 14, 2008.

Book, Eric. E-mail interview with the author. January 28, 2008.

Bronson, Po. "Learning to Lie." *New York,* February 10, 2008. 34+.

Buck, Pearl S. *To My Daughters, with Love.* New York: John Day, 1967. Reprinted in *Building Character in Schools*, by Kevin Ryan and Karen E. Bohlin. San Francisco: Jossey-Bass, 2003. 46.

Buffett, Warren. "A Conversation with Warren Buffett." Interview with Carol J. Loomis. *Fortune,* June 25, 2006. Available online. URL: http://www.cnnmoney.com. Accessed February 8, 2008.

Cesar E. Chavez Foundation. "An American Hero." Available online. URL: http://www.chavezfoundation.org/ cesarchavez.html. Accessed February 27, 2008.

Clarey, Christopher. "ATLANTA: DAY 5—GYMNASTICS; for the Magnificent Seven, It Hurts So Good." *The New York Times,* July 24, 1996. Available online. URL: http://www.nytimes. com. Accessed March 15, 2008.

Corporation for National and Community Service, and U.S. Census Bureau. "Fact Sheet on 'Service-Learning, School-Based Service, and Civic Engagement.'" *Youth Volunteering and Civic Engagement Survey.* April 2007. Available online.

URL: http://www.nationalservice.gov/about/role_impact/
performance_research.asp#YHA. Accessed March 14, 2008.

Covey, Sean. *The 7 Habits of Highly Effective Teens*. New York:
Fireside, 1998.

"Daniel Boone." *Today in History*. Library of Congress. Available online. URL: http://memory.loc.gov/today/jun07.html.
February 23, 2008.

Davis, Ronald L.F. "Creating Jim Crow." *The History of Jim Crow*.
PBS. Available online. URL: http://www.jimcrowhistory.
org/history/creating2.htm. Accessed March 15, 2008.

Department of Health and Human Services, Centers for Disease Control and Prevention. "Trends in the Prevalence of
Selected Risk Behaviors." *National Youth Risk Behavior Survey: 1991–2007*. YRBSS. Available online. URL: http://www.
cdc.gov/yrbss. Accessed February 11, 2008.

The Devil Came on Horseback. 2007. DVD. Break Thru Films.

Didion, Joan. "On Self Respect." *Slouching Toward Bethlehem*.
New York: Farrar, Straus and Giroux, 1990.

Druskat, Vanessa Urch, and Steven B. Wolff. "Building the
Emotional Intelligence of Groups." *Harvard Business Review*
(March 2001). Reprinted in *Harvard Business Review on
Teams That Succeed*. Boston: Harvard Business School,
2004. 27–51.

Dunham, Will. "Study Finds U.S. Music Awash in Booze and
Drugs." *Reuters,* February 4, 2008. Available online. URL:
http://www.reuters.com/articlePrint?articleID=USN0144737
220080204. Accessed February 11, 2008.

Evans, Nikole. Y2kyouth.org. 2008. Available online. URL:
http://www.y2kyouth.org. Accessed March 15, 2008.

———. E-mail interview with the author. February 11, 2008.

"The Four Helpers." The Official Anne Frank House Web site.
Available online. URL: http://www.annefrank.org/content.
asp?pid=2&lid=2. Accessed March 14, 2008.

Frank, Anne. *Anne Frank: The Diary of a Young Girl*. New York:
Bantam, 1993.

Gies, Miep. "Miep Gies Remembers Anne Frank." Interview with Menno Metselaar. Official Anne Frank House Web site. 1998. Transcript. Available online. URL: http://www.annefrank. org/content.asp?PID=242&LID=2. Accessed March 14, 2008.

Global Health Council. Available online. URL: http://www. globalhealth.org. Accessed March 15, 2008.

Goleman, Daniel. "Free Won't: The Marshmallow Test Revisited." Weblog entry. August 24, 2007. DanielGoleman.info. Available online. URL: http://www.danielgoleman.info/blog. Accessed March 26, 2008.

"The Google Culture." Google Corporate Information. Available online. URL: http://www.google.com/corporate/culture. html. Accessed March 15, 2008.

Grohmann, Karolos. "IOC Strips Marion Jones' Sydney Medals." *Reuters,* December 12, 2007. Available online. URL: http:// www.reuters.com. Accessed March 14, 2008.

Gutman, Dan. *Jackie & Me*. New York: HarperCollins, 2000.

Heilemann, John. "Steve Jobs in a Box." *New York,* July 18, 2007. Available online. URL: http://nymag.com/news/ features/33524/. Accessed March 15, 2008.

Hohenadel, Kristen. "An Animated Adventure, Drawn from Life." *New York Times,* January 21, 2007. Available online. URL: http://www.nytimes.com. Accessed February 9, 2008.

Howe, Randy, ed. *Coachisms: Winning Words from the Country's Finest Coaches*. Guilford, Conn.: Globe Pequot, 2005. 49.

Hurricane Katrina: Rebuilding the Gulf Coast Region. White House. Available online. URL: http://www.whitehouse.gov/ infocus/katrina/. Accessed March 15, 2008.

"International Space Station." NASA. Available online. URL: http://www.nasa.gov/mission_pages/station/main/index. html. Accessed March 15, 2008.

Jefferson, Thomas. "Transcript: Jefferson's Instructions for Meriwether Lewis." Letter to Meriwether Lewis, June 20, 1803. *Rivers, Edens, Empires: Lewis & Clark and the Revealing of America*, edited by George W. Gawalt. Washington,

D.C.: LC, 2006. *Lewis & Clark.* Library of Congress, Washington. Available online. URL: http://www.loc.gov/exhibits/lewisandclark/transcript57.html. Accessed March 15, 2008.

Johnson, Troy, Dr. "We Hold the Rock: The Alcatraz Indian Occupation." Alcatraz Island. October 2, 2007. National Parks Service, U.S. Department of the Interior. Available online. URL: http://www.nps.gov/alca/historyculture/we-hold-the-rock.htm. Accessed February 26, 2008.

"Jones (six months), Former Coach (63 months) Sentence to Prison." *Associated Press,* January 11, 2008. Available online. URL: http://www.ap.org. Accessed March 14, 2008.

Jordan, Michael, and Janet Lowe. *Michael Jordan Speaks: Lessons from the World's Greatest Champion.* New York: Wiley, 1999.

Katzenbach, Jon R., and Douglas K. Smith. "The Discipline of Teams." *Harvard Business Review* (March 1993). Reprinted in *Harvard Business Review on Teams That Succeed.* Boston: Harvard Business School, 2004. 1–25.

Keller, Helen. "Alone can do so little; Together we can do so much." *The Book of Positive Quotations.* Compiled by John Cook. Minneapolis, Minn.: Fairview Press, 2007. 618.

Kidder, Rushworth M. *"There's Only Ethics."* Institute for Global Ethics. Available online. URL: www.globalethics.org/resources/pdf/pl_2000_01.pdf.

King, Martin Luther, Jr. Address to MIA Mass Meeting. Martin Luther King, Jr. Research and Education Institute. Holt Street Baptist Church. November 14, 1956. Reprinted in *The Papers of Martin Luther King, Jr.* Available online. URL: http://www.stanford.edu/group/King/publications/papers/vol3/561114.013-Address_to_MIA_Mass_Meeting_at_Holt_Street_Baptist_Church.htm. Accessed March 15, 2008.

Kolata, Gina. "A Suprising Secret to a Long Life: Stay in School." *The New York Times,* January 3, 2007. Available online. URL: http://www.nytimes.com. Accessed February 11, 2008.

Lashinsky, Adam. "Can Google Three-peat?" *Fortune,* January 31, 2008. Available online. URL: http://cnnmoney.com. Accessed March 15, 2008.

Lewis, Barbara A. *What Do You Stand For? For Teens: A Guide to Building Character.* Minneapolis: Free Spirit, 2005.

Lickona, Thomas. *Character Matters.* New York: Simon & Schuster, 2004.

———. *Educating for Character: How Our Schools Can Teach Respect and Responsibility.* New York: Bantam, 1991.

"The Life of Henry Ford." The Henry Ford Museum. 2003. Available online. URL: http://www.hfmgv.org/exhibits/hf/. Accessed March 15, 2008.

"Living the Legacy: The Women's Rights Movement 1848–1998." *Legacy '98.* 2002. National Women's History Project. Available online. URL: http://www.legacy98.org/move-hist.html. Accessed March 15, 2008.

Loomis, Carol J. "Warren Buffet Gives Away His Fortune." *Fortune,* June 25, 2006. Available online. URL: http://cnnmoney.com. Accessed February 8, 2008.

Lowery, Ava. *Peace Takes Courage.* February 23, 2008. Available online. URL: http://www.peacetakescourage.com. Accessed March 15, 2008.

Lumpkin, Bernard. "Teen Blogger for Peace Ava Lowrey: You Need to Know Me." MTV News. July 3, 2007. Available online. URL: http://mtv.com/news/articles/1564000/20070703/index.jhtml#. Accessed March 14, 2008.

Lupica, Mike. "Eli Manning, David Tyree Show Why Giants are Super This Night." New York *Daily News.* February 4, 2008. Available online. URL: http://www.nydailynews.com. Accessed March 15, 2008.

Macavinta, Courtney, and Andrea Vander Pluym. *Respect: A Girl's Guide to Getting Respect & Dealing When Your Line Is Crossed.* Minneapolis, Minn.: Free Spirit, 2005.

MacGillis, Alec. "Obama's Private Idaho." Weblog entry. February 2, 2008. The Trail: A Diary of Campaign 2008. Available online. URL: http://blog.washingtonpost.com/

the-trail/2008/02/02/obamas_private_idaho.html. Accessed March 15, 2008.

Mankiller, Wilma, and Michael Wallis. *Mankiller: A Chief and Her People.* New York: Macmillan, 1994.

"Maya Lin Biography." *Art: 21.* 2007. PBS. Available online. URL: http://www.pbs.org/art21/artists/lin/index.html. Accessed March 15, 2008.

McFadden, Robert D. "Edmund Hillary, First on Everest, Dies at 88." *New York Times,* January 10, 2008. Available online. URL: http://www.nytimes.com. Accessed March 15, 2008.

Mead, Margaret. Introduction. *The World Ahead: An Anthropologist Anticipates the Future.* New York: Berghahn Books, 2005. 12.

Menard, Anthony. E-mail interview with the author. February 7, 2008.

"Michael Jordan Bio." NBA.com. 2008. Available online. URL: http://www.nba.com/playerfile/michael_jordan/bio.html. Accessed March 15, 2008.

Mitchell, George J. "Executive Summary." *Report to the Commissioner of Baseball of an Independent Investigation into the Illegal Use of Steroids and Other Performance Enhancing Substances by Player in Major League Baseball. Major League Baseball.* December 13, 2007. DLA Piper US LLP. Available online. URL: http://mlb.mlb.com/mlb/news/mitchell/index.jsp. Accessed March 14, 2008.

MK Level Playing Field Institute. "Executive Summary." *HOWFAIR Study.* 2003. Available online. URL: http://www.lpfi.org/workplace/howfair.shtml. Accessed March 14, 2008.

"Mohandas Gandhi (1869–1948)." BBC History. Available online. URL: http://www.bbc.co.uk/history/historic_figures/gandhi_mohandas.shtml. Accessed March 14, 2008.

Moreira, Naila F. "Inventing by Trial, Error, and Teamwork." *Boston Globe,* June 16, 2006. Available online. URL: http://www.boston.com. Accessed March 14, 2008.

Murphy, Madonna. *Character Education in America's Blue Ribbon Schools.* Lanham, Md.: Scarecrow Press, 2002.

National Center for Educational Statistics. *Youth Indicators 2005: Trends in the Well-Being of American Youth.* U.S. Department of Education, Institute of Education Sciences. Available online. URL: http://nces.ed.gov/pubsearch/pubsinfo.asp?pubid=2005050. Accessed March 14, 2008.

Nelson, Andrew. "Wilma Mankiller." Salon.com. November 20, 2001. Available online. URL: http://archive.salon.com/people/bc/2001/11/20/mankiller/index.html?source=search&aim=/people/bc. Accessed March 15, 2008.

"1996 U.S. Women's Gymnastics Team." U.S. Olympic Hall of Fame. Available online. URL: http://www.usolympichalloffame.com/?page_id=37. Accessed March 15, 2008.

The Official Web site of Vince Lombardi. Available online. URL: http://vincelombardi.com/. Accessed March 15, 2008.

"100 Best Companies to Work for 2008." *Fortune,* February 4, 2008. Available online. URL: http://money.cnn.com/magazines/fortune/bestcompanies/2008/. Accessed March 15, 2008.

"One Hundred Years Toward Suffrage: An Overview." *National American Woman Suffrage Association Collection.* Library of Congress. Available online. URL: http://memory.loc.gov/ammem/naw/nawstime.html. Accessed March 15, 2008.

One: The Campaign to Make Poverty History. Available online. URL: http://www.one.org. Accessed March 15, 2008.

"On This Day 1989: Massacre in Tiananmen Square." *BBC News,* June 4, 1989. Available online. URL: http://news.bbc.co.uk. Accessed March 14, 2008.

Oppedisano, Dana. "Class 3A State Champions: Naples' 'Unremarkable' Seniors Win It All." *Naples Daily News,* December 14, 2007. Available online. URL: http://naplesnews.com/news/2007/dec/14/class-3a-state-champions-naples-unremarkable-senio/. Accessed March 15, 2008.

PBS. "Transcontinental Railroad." *American Experience.* Available online. URL: http://www.pbs.org/wgbh/amex/tcrr/. Accessed February 23, 2008.

————. "TR's Legacy: The Panama Canal." *TR, the Story of Theo-dore Roosevelt.* Available online. URL: http://www.pbs.org/wgbh/amex/tr/panama.html. Accessed February 23, 2008.

Polgreen, Lydia. "Scorched-Earth Strategy Returns to Darfur." *New York Times,* March 2, 2008. Available online. URL: http://www.nytimes.com. Accessed March 15, 2008.

Powell, Colin. *My American Journey.* New York: Random House, 1995.

Preston, William. Letter to George Washington. January 31, 1775. *The George Washington Papers at the Library of Congress, 1741–1799,* edited by Stanislaus Murray Hamilton. New York: Society of the Colonial Dames of America, 1898. *American Memory.* Library of Congress, Washington. Available online. URL: http://memory.loc.gov. Accessed February 23, 2008.

Quick Stats: Underage Drinking. Centers for Disease Control and Prevention. Available online. URL: http://www.cdc.gov/alcohol/quickstats/underage_drinking.htm. Accessed February 11, 2008.

"Red Sox Championship Commemorative Section." *Boston Globe,* October 27, 2004. Available online. URL: http://www.boston.com/sports/baseball/redsox/articles/2004/10/31/commemorative/. Accessed March 15, 2008.

Ryan, Kevin, and Karen E. Bohlin. *Building Character in Schools: Practical Ways to Bring Moral Instruction to Life.* San Francisco: Jossey-Bass, 2003.

Satrapi, Marjane. *The Complete Persepolis.* Translated by L'Association and Anjali Singh. New York: Pantheon-Random, 2003.

"The Seneca Falls Convention, July 19–20, 1848." National Portrait Gallery, Smithsonian Institute. Available online. URL: http://www.npg.si.edu/col/seneca/senfalls1.htm. Accessed March 15, 2008.

Shaw, George Bernard. "Without good manners human society becomes intolerable and impossible." *Wisdom Through the Ages.* Compiled by Helen Granat. N.p.: Trafford, 2003. 178.

Smale, Will. "Profile: The Google Founders." *BBC News,* April 30, 2004. Available online. URL: http://news.bbc.co.uk/2/hi/business/3666241.stm. Accessed March 15, 2008.

"A Statue Unveiled of Woods' Father, a Moment Worth a Fist Pump." *Golf,* January 21, 2008. Available online. URL: http://www.golf.com/golf/tours_news/article/0,28136,1705643,00.html. Accessed March 15, 2008.

Steidle, Brian. "In Darfur, My Camera Was Not Nearly Enough." *Washington Post,* March 20, 2005. Available online. URL: http://www.washingtonpost.com. Accessed March 15, 2008.

"Steve Jobs." Apple Inc. Available online. URL: http://www.apple.com/pr/bios/jobs.html. Accessed March 15, 2008.

StopGlobalWarming.org. March 13, 2008. Available online. URL: http://www.stopglobalwarming.org. Accessed March 15, 2008.

"'Summer of Soul' Melded Music, Cultural Change." NPR Music. Available online. URL: http://www.npr.org/templates/story/story.php?storyId=12119916. Accessed March 15, 2008.

Tartaglia, Louis. *Flawless! The Ten Most Common Character Flaws and What You Can Do About Them.* New York: Quill, 1999. Reprinted in *Character Matters*, by Thomas Lickona. New York: Simon & Schuster, 2004. 11.

The Nobel Foundation. "Lech Walesa: The Nobel Peace Prize 1983." Nobelprize.org. Available online. URL: http://nobelprize.org/nobel_prizes/peace/laureates/1983/walesa-bio.html. Accessed March 14, 2008.

"Thomas Alva Edison (1847–1931)." *American Memory.* Library of Congress. Available online. URL: http://memory.loc.gov/ammem/edhtml/edbiohm.html. Accessed March 15, 2008.

UN in Brief. United Nations. Available online. URL: http://www.un.org/Overview/uninbrief. Accessed March 15, 2008.

Urban, Hal. *20 Things I Want My Kids to Know: Passing on Life's Greatest Lessons.* Nashville, Tenn.: Thomas Nelson, 1992.

"Venus and Serena Williams." *Sports Illustrated Scrapbook.* SportsIllustrated.com. Available online. URL: http://

sportsillustrated.cnn.com/tennis/features/williams/main/. Accessed March 15, 2008.

Vietnam Veterans Memorial. August 23, 2007. National Parks Service. Available online. URL: http://www.nps.gov/vive/. Accessed March 15, 2008.

Williams, Juan. "A Hispanic Civil Rights Movement." *Washington Post,* April 10, 2006. Available online. URL: http://www. washingtonpost.com. Accessed February 27, 2008.

"Wright Brothers History." Wright House. Available online. URL: http://www.wright-house.com/wright-brothers/Wrights. html. Accessed March 15, 2008.

"WTA Player Profile: Serena Williams." Tennis.com. March 10, 2008. Available online. URL: http://www.tennis.com/ players/wta/profiles/swilliams.aspx?id=15482. Accessed March 15, 2008.

"WTA Player Profile: Venus Williams." Tennis.com. January 16, 2008. Available online. URL: http://www.tennis.com/ players/wta/profiles/vwilliams.aspx?id=10980. Accessed March 15, 2008.

FURTHER RESOURCES

BOOKS

Bachel, Beverly K. *What Do You Really Want? How to Set a Goal and Go for It: A Guide for Teens.* Minneapolis, Minn.: Free Spirit Publishing, 2001.

Covey, Sean. *The 6 Most Important Decisions You'll Ever Make: A Guide for Teens.* New York: Simon & Schuster, 2006.

David, Laurie, and Cambria Gordon. *The Down-to-Earth Guide to Global Warming.* New York: Scholastic, 2007.

Frank, Anne. *Anne Frank: Diary of a Young Girl.* New York: Bantam, 1993.

Macavinta, Courtney, and Andrea Vander Pluym. *Respect: A Girl's Guide to Getting Respect & Dealing When Your Line Is Crossed.* Minneapolis, Minn.: Free Spirit Publishing, 2005.

Senning, Cindy Post, and Peggy Post. *Teen Manners: From Malls to Messaging and Beyond.* New York: HarperCollins, 2007.

WEB SITES

Teen Central
www.teencentral.net
Get advice about any topic anonymously from adult professionals.

Do Something
www.dosomething.org
Connect to issues you care about and do something to help in your community.

Youth at Work
www.youth.eeoc.gov
Find out about your rights and responsibilities as an employee.

PICTURE CREDITS

INDEX

ABOUT THE AUTHOR AND CONSULTANTS

Tara Welty has more than eight years of experience as an educational writer and editor, contributing to Scholastic Inc., Macmillan/McGraw-Hill, Pearson, and Harcourt. She has an M.A. in Playwriting and Theater History from New York University's Gallatin School of Individualized Study. Tara's writing career began at age 14 when she drafted a spirited "Letter to the Editor" to her local newspaper demanding respect for teenagers. Welty and her husband, from whom she has learned a lot about teamwork, live in Brooklyn, New York, with two cats.

Series consultant **Dr. Madonna Murphy** is a professor of education at the University of St. Francis in Joliet, Illinois, where she teaches education and character education courses to teachers. She is the author of *Character Education in America's Blue Ribbon Schools* and *History & Philosophy of Education: Voices of Educational Pioneers*. She has served as the character education consultant for a series of more than 40 character education books for elementary school children, on the Character Education Partnership's Blue Ribbon Award committee recognizing K-12 schools for their character education, and on a national committee for promoting character education in teacher education institutions.

Series consultant **Sharon L. Banas** was a middle school teacher in Amherst and Tonawanda, New York, for more than 30 years. She led the Sweet Home Central School District in the development of its nationally acclaimed character education program. In 1992, Sharon was a member of the Aspen Conference, drafting the Aspen Declaration that was approved by the U.S. Congress. In 2001, she published *Caring Messages for a School Year*. She has been married to her husband Doug for 37 years. They have a daughter, son, and new granddaughter.